PROFESSIONAL ISSUES IN EDUCATION

NUMBER SIXTEEN

5–14: SCOTLAND'S NATIONAL CURRICULUM

PROFESSIONAL ISSUES IN EDUCATION

1: Gordon Kirk, *Teacher Education and Professional Development.*
2: Sally Brown (editor), *Assessment: A Changing Practice.*
3: John MacBeath, *Personal and Social Education.*
4: A. Douglas Weir, *Education and Vocation: 14-18.*
5: W. A. Gatherer, *Curriculum Development in Scotland.*
6: C. Harrison and M. Macintosh, *Managing Change: The Head Teacher's Perspectives.*
7: Robert Glaister (editor), *Studies of Promoted Posts.*
8: Helen Penn, *Under Fives: The View from Strathclyde.*
9: Joyce Watt, *Early Education: The Current Debate.*
10: Alastair Macbeth, *School Boards: From Purpose to Practice.*
11: David Hartley and Angela Roger (editors), *Curriculum and Assessment in Scotland: A Policy for the 90s.*
12: Ian C. M. Fairweather and J.N. MacDonald, *Religious Education.*
13: Gordon Kirk and Robert Glaister (editors), *Scottish Education and the European Community.*
14: David Hartley, *Teacher Appraisal - A Policy Analysis.*
15: Joyce Watt (editor), *Early Education: The Quality Debate*
16: Gordon Kirk and Robert Glaister (editors), *5–14: Scotland's National Curriculum*

PROFESSIONAL ISSUES IN EDUCATION

GORDON KIRK *editors* ROBERT GLAISTER

5–14: SCOTLAND'S NATIONAL CURRICULUM

edited by
GORDON KIRK
AND
ROBERT GLAISTER

with contributions from
Frank Adams   Don Skinner
Alan Macdonald   Sally Brown
David Carr

SCOTTISH ACADEMIC PRESS
EDINBURGH

Published by
Scottish Academic Press
56 Hanover Street, Edinburgh EH2 2DX

© 1994 Scottish Academic Press Ltd

First published 1994
ISBN 0 7073 0740 6

All rights reserved. No part of this publication may be reproduced, stored in a retrieval system, or transmitted, in any form or by any means, electronic, mechanical, photocopying, recording or otherwise, without the prior permission of Scottish Academic Press Ltd.

British Library Cataloguing in Publication data

A catalogue record of this book is available from the British Library.

Typeset by Trinity Typesetting, Edinburgh.

CONTENTS

Editorial Introduction — vii

The Authors — x

1 **5–14: Framework and Context**
   Frank Adams — 1

2 **5–14: Modes of Teaching**
   Don Skinner — 26

3 **5–14: Themes and Subjects**
   Alan Macdonald — 50

4 **5–14: Assessment and Testing**
   Sally Brown — 69

5 **5–14: A Philosophical Critique**
   David Carr — 87

   Appendix 1: Curriculum Areas in 5–14
   Development Programme — 102

   Appendix 2: 5–14 Development Programme
   Materials — 111

EDITORIAL INTRODUCTION

The title of this series intends to signal its three main features. Firstly, its general area is education. That term, however, means more than schooling, more than a narrowly instrumental view of a process, and extends beyond the limited notion of an institutional base for activities. Secondly, the topics chosen are matters which excite a good deal of interest and concern, mainly, but not exclusively, because they involve change and development. They are matters on which widely differing views are held: in that sense they are issues. Finally, the series will explore ideas and principles which relate directly to educational practice and to the context in which practices are developed and debated. In that sense the issues raised are professional.

The last few years have seen very significant developments in Scottish education. Much change has taken place so quickly that the process of development has been masked. Equally, practitioners are so busy with the implementation of change in their own practice that they are unaware of developments around the country. If the full benefit from change is to be realised, it is necessary to feed both review and analysis of the process and the product back into the system. This series is an attempt to realise that objective.

The topics will be issues which arise in Scotland, are of critical concern in Scotland, but which will be documented and discussed in a way which makes them equally accessible to an audience furth of Scotland. Indeed, each volume is intended to contribute to the wider educational debate and to inform and enliven the critical discussion of changes in educational practice in Britain and elsewhere. The series should not be seen as a collection of research reports, but rather each volume should draw on research findings and other appropriate resources to offer a readable, lively and rigorous analysis of the issues involved.

One of the justifications for the establishment of the Professional Issues in Education series was to rectify the tendency for educational developments in Scotland to be under-documented and, partly for that reason, to be insufficiently exposed to critical discussion. The 5–14 Development Programme has been a massive initiative, originating in ministerial concerns about national standards in Scottish schools and the coherence of the curriculum and its assessment. An earlier volume in this series – Curriculum and Assessment in Scotland, edited by Hartley and Roger – provided a policy analysis of the central consultation paper *Curriculum and Assessment in Scotland: A Policy for the 1990s*. Since that volume appeared in 1990, the National Development Programme has proceeded apace. A number of Review and Development Groups were established to review good practice. Each of these groups developed draft guidelines, which were then the focus of widespread consultation amongst teachers and others. The draft guidelines were subsequently revised and issued with the standing of national guidelines. It is important to note that, while these are not legally binding on schools, they are issued with the authority of the Secretary of State for Scotland and are being universally adopted in Scottish schools. A comprehensive set of official documents covering the whole initiative are now available in the public domain and, indeed, have been widely disseminated throughout Scottish schools.

It is therefore possible for that major piece of national curriculum development to be open to critical scrutiny and, since that is one of the primary functions of the series, it is reasonable to consider the initiative in its entirety.

The contributors to this volume offer a range of contrasting perspectives. Alan Macdonald writes as a practising headteacher; Don Skinner writes as someone who was a member of one of the Review and Development Groups; Frank Adams is heavily involved in the professional education of teachers; Professor Sally Brown brings her own professional expertise and authority in the field of assessment to consider the way in which assessment is handled in the initiative; and, finally, David Carr offers a philosophical critique of the thinking underpinning the initiative. These contrasting and complementary perspectives contribute to a volume that will be of interest to practising teachers, teachers in training, others concerned with curriculum development and its management in Scotland as well as students of the national curriculum in other countries. It therefore is an important contribution to the Professional Issues in Education series.

Professor Gordon Kirk *Principal,*
Moray House Institute of Education

Dr Robert Glaister *Dean,*
Faculty of Education, The Open University

THE AUTHORS

FRANK ADAMS is Head of Primary Education, Moray House Institute of Education

DON SKINNER is Senior Lecturer in Primary Education, Moray House Institute of Education

ALAN MACDONALD is Headteacher of Donibristle Primary School, Dalgety Bay, Fife

SALLY BROWN is Professor of Education, University of Stirling

DAVID CARR is Reader in Education, Moray House Institute of Education

CHAPTER 1

5–14: FRAMEWORK AND CONTEXT

Frank Adams

Introduction – the 1987 Consultative Paper

The Curriculum and Assessment 5–14 programme was launched by the Secretary of State for Scotland with the publication, in 1987, of the consultation paper *Curriculum and Assessment in Scotland: A Policy for the 1990s* (SED 1987), which expressed concern over a number of perceived weaknesses in the school system for 5–14 year olds. These weaknesses were identified as

> (i) ... substantial variation in the nature and quality of curriculum planning and management; (ii) lack of definition of the curriculum; (iii) progress in primary and the early years of secondary school; (iv) curricular discontinuity, especially in the four years between P6 and S2; (v) inconsistency of approaches to assessment and (vi) poor communication with parents (SED 1987: 7).

The proposed response to the identified weaknesses was to be a programme of action intended to achieve a number of ends:

> (i) clearer definition ... of the content and objectives of the curriculum; (ii) the establishment and implementation of satisfactory assessment policies in all schools, an integral part of which will be a requirement to assess children in certain key skills on a nationally standardised basis; (iii) better communi-

cation between schools and parents on the curriculum and assessment policies and practices of the school and better reporting on the progress of pupils; (iv) consistent application in schools of the nationally agreed approach to curriculum and assessment matters (SED 1987:4).

The Secretary of State's consultative paper has already been the subject of substantial comment and analysis in an earlier volume in this series, *Curriculum and Assessment in Scotland: A Policy for the 1990s* (Hartley and Rodger 1990), in which considerable doubts and concerns regarding the effects of the 5–14 Programme on Scottish teachers and Scottish education were expressed. Among these doubts and concerns, often relating to the political motives behind the 5–14 Programme, there is, however, a recognition that pupils in Scottish schools do have a right or entitlement to an educational experience which is of high quality and which has a degree of consistency across the country. David Robertson, for example, says

> Curriculum management and planning are patchy and it is right that we should seek to bring all schools up to the standards of the best' (Robertson in Rodger and Hartley, 1990:85).

The issue, of course, remains as to how what is 'best' is identified and whether the developments that have taken place in the six years since the publication of the SED's consultative paper are likely to improve quality or whether they have confirmed that the 5–14 initiative is indeed the 'epitaph for progressive primary education' predicted by David Hartley (in Rodger and Hartley, 1990:103).

The 5–14 Development Programme is now at a stage where all of the curriculum advice and guidance documents and the material on assessment and reporting have been published in their final form and it is possible to reflect on how the Programme has developed since its launch in 1987.

5–14 – A new rationale for Scottish education?

Prior to the 5–14 programme, the only attempt to produce a rationale linking primary and secondary was that of the Education 10–14 Programme. The rationale suggested in Education 10–14 (CCC 1986) to give coherence and continuity to the educational experience from primary stages into and through the secondary stages did not meet with favour in the eyes of the SOED. Given that was the case, it might have been expected that a new and more acceptable rationale would have been published by SOED in place of the apparently deficient 10–14 rationale. An attempt by the new SCCC, successor to the CCC, to develop a full statement on primary education in 1987 met with no more success than that of the 10–14 Programme. The primary rationale, presented to the SOED, resulted in a much edited and reduced statement, lacking any sense of academic or professional rigour, which was published as Working Paper No. 1 'The Balance of the Primary Curriculum' (SOED 1987) launching the Curriculum and Assessment 5–14 programme. An intense concern to force an arithmetic form of 'balance' on the primary curriculum in order to form a link with its secondary counterpart (SCCC, 1989) meant that the thinking which was essential for the subsequent work of Review and Development Groups was never carried out.

A Curriculum framework without a rationale?

The overarching concerns of the 5–14 Development Programme have been continuity, progression and structure. The structure is set out in Working Paper No 1 encompassing five curriculum areas for the primary stages, *Language, Mathematics, Environmental Studies, Expressive Arts, Religious and Moral Education, and Personal and Social Development.* The 5–14 Programme's first challenge was to establish a link to the eight modes which had been identified as the curriculum structure for the secondary stages at S3 and beyond. These modes are *Language and Communication, Mathematical Studies and Applications, Scientific Studies and Applications, Social and Environmental Studies, Technological Studies and Applications, Creative and Aesthetic Activities, Physical Education, and Religious and Moral Education.*

This guidance on curriculum structure maintained the established breadth in the curriculum at both the primary and secondary stages up to S4. A problem, however, for the 5–14 programme was that of finding a structure which also dealt with the issue of breadth in the curriculum. The meaning of the term 'a balanced curriculum' in the primary context was alleged by critics to be unclear principally because primary practice, since the late 1960s, had been to reject the need for an explicitly timetabled curriculum, unlike practice in the secondary context. The flexibility of primary provision had long been argued for as a source of strength in its ability to allow teachers to respond to childrens' learning but that same flexibility was also regarded by critics as a barrier to understanding what goes on in primary schools and to communicating with parents and secondary schools. The importance placed by Government in the early 1980s on parental choice in education and on parental access to information about their children meant that priority was given within the Curriculum and Assessment 5–14 Programme to clearing up this apparent barrier to communication.

The solution found to the problem was to devise a set of time allocations for the various areas of the primary curriculum and to relate them to time allocations already agreed for dealing with the eight modes in the timetable of the first two years of secondary school. This advice, first published in Working Paper No. 1 (SED 1989) and elaborated in the final guidelines (SOED June 1993) is set out in figure 1 below.

FIGURE 1
Balance of Allocation of Time in Year 5–14

PRIMARY

LANGUAGE	MATHEMATICS	ENV. STUDIES	EXPRESSIVE ARTS	RELIGIOUS AND MORAL EDUCATION	FLEXIBILITY
15%	15%	25%	15%	10%	20%

SECONDARY

LANG. & COMMUN.	MATH. STUDIES & APPL.	SCIENTIFIC STUD. & APPL.	SOCIAL & ENVIRON. STUDIES	TECHN. ACTIV. & APPL.	CREATIVE & AESTH. ACTIVITY	PHYS. EDUCATION	RELIG. & MORAL EDUC.	FLEXIBILITY
20%	10%	10%	10%	10%	10%	5%	5%	20%

The time allocations for primary, while understandable in basic terms, do little to address some of the overall principles underlying primary provision. For example, the designation of a set time allocation for Language does not, overtly at least, acknowledge the significant language development that can take place in contexts in other curricular areas. This kind of problem had been recognised by the authors of 'Primary Education in the Eighties' (COPE 1983) when they accepted that any definition of balance in the primary curriculum has to go beyond simple arithmetic calculations of hours. The guidance within the 5–14 Programme given to teachers and headteachers on this issue does at least recognise that handling fixed time allocations in the primary school can be problematic and that the timetabling arrangements of secondary can be a barrier to the development of understanding across the curriculum.

> Achievement of balance is not necessarily realised by adherence to the time allocations ... on a week by week basis. The headteacher will monitor the overall balance by attention to each area of the curriculum throughout a pupil's education. Primary teachers should monitor and maintain an appropriate balance throughout the year ... Together with their headteacher they should review regularly, at least each term the balance which has been achieved. In secondary schools, balance in the curriculum will, to a large extent, be secured through appropriate timetabling arrangements. However the secondary teacher should be conscious of the extent to which study in one subject or area of the curriculum can contribute to pupils' development in another when appropriate links have been established (SOED June 1993, p. 17).

The flexibility allowance is suggested at both the primary and secondary stages as a way of dealing with specific concerns of individual schools, particular curricular areas or activities at different stages of the school:

> This flexibility time can also be used for dealing with cross-curricular aspects; for learning support and enrichment; for

pastoral care; for whole school activities; or for opportunities for learning which may arise from contemporary events or issues. Schools should therefore consider how best to use this important element (SOED June 1993, p. 17).

The publication of the Working Paper (SED 1989) was directly followed by the setting up of six Review and Development Groups (RDGs) with the remit to review and make proposals on the curriculum content and programmes of study for the years 5–14 in English Language, Mathematics, Environmental Studies, Expressive Arts, Religious and Moral Education, and Personal and Social Development. A further three groups were set up to consider Developing the Whole Curriculum 5–14, Assessment and Testing, and Reporting. It is interesting to note that the latter two groups were set up under the auspices of the SOED rather than the SCCC which was responsible for the other RDGs. A number of task groups were also set up within the Language area on Latin, Modern European Languages in S1 and S2, and on Gaelic 5–14. Appendix 1 sets out the details of the curriculum structure which was developed within each of the RDGs and task groups.

The curriculum structure within which the RDGs were expected to work concentrates centrally on the identification of *outcomes and strands* (the curricular framework), *targets* (specific learning goals) and *levels* (attainment targets grouped at 5 levels of progression from A–E). The rationale for each curriculum area receives very little attention and the inclusion of a section called 'Programmes of Study', directly related to the five levels of attainment, makes it evident that there is little overall rationale for the Development programme other than to achieve the central principles of 5–14, namely breadth, balance, coherence, continuity and progression within an overall assessment focussed context.

There is little doubt that these central principles are extremely important, especially in the transition from primary schools to secondaries but the lack of any sustained argument for the adoption of this approach in preference to a less fragmented, more child-centred approach makes its validity less persuasive. The existence of terms such as balance, continuity, progression and differentiation seem to suggest that the only sensible approach is to ensure that clear subject guidelines are laid down with specific targets and clear assessment. However, this represents only one view of curriculum structure and the case has not been made to convince many, especially in the field of primary education, that this is the only correct view. No acknowledgement exists within the 5–14 Programme that it might be possible to conceptualise learning outcomes differently, for example with much more emphasis on the learner and a much more flexible role for the teacher.

The practical, as well as conceptual, problem of the 5–14 Programme's approach is that it seems to imply that children can be regarded as being somehow homogeneous and it ignores the difficulties caused by the fact that children will progress at different rates at different times across different curricular areas. Similar experiences with the Standard Grade developments and the problems created for teachers of structuring curriculum and assessment tasks across a range of grade-related criteria suggest that the lessons are there for the curriculum developers to learn. The need for a substantial programme of support for primary teachers in meeting a task which is at least the equal of that of Standard Grade seems clear and has become especially acute in the light of growing concerns over the workload of teachers. This issue will be returned to later in the context of the implementation of the 5–14 Programme.

5–14 National Guidelines – Central Control or Professional Consensus?

The lack of an overall statement of philosophy for the 5–

14 Programme led to concerns on the part of teachers and others, that the National Guidelines would signal a return to pre-Primary Memorandum (SED 1965) attitudes. This did not appear to be borne out by the first publications of the 5–14 Programme, the draft report of Review and Development Group (RDG) 1 on English Language 5–14 (SOED March 1990) and the final National Guidelines, Language 5–14 (SOED June 1991). Responses from the profession to the Language guidelines and subsequently to the report of RDG 2 on Mathematics 5–14 (SOED May 1990; SOED August 1991) seemed to suggest that the 5–14 Programme was perhaps not going to be as educationally suspect as many had feared and that much of what had been regarded as being 'good practice' in these curricular areas would be endorsed by the new National Guidelines. The view began to be expressed that the decision to use the SCCC and a system of Review and Development Groups, involving both primary and secondary practitioners, had to some extent drawn the teeth of the original consultative paper and that the Scottish version of the 'National' Curriculum would find more favour among Scottish practitioners than its counterpart appeared to be winning in England and Wales. This apparent agreement, however, masks the fact that voices hostile to the models of language and mathematics learning presented in the draft documents were raised during the consultation period although there is little evidence of any heed being taken of them in the move to the final versions of these guidelines.

Not far behind this apparently easy consensus lay an uneasy tension between the structuring of individual, discrete subjects such as Mathematics or Language and that of the loose coalition of other curricular areas. Art, Music, Drama and Physical Education, for example, remained grouped as Expressive Arts in the 5–14 Programme. (It might be recalled that the term Expressive Arts emerged in the mid-80s without any extended justification even then.) An even greater tension existed within the area of Environmental Studies where the needs of the discrete subjects of history, geography, science, and those of other areas such as health, home economics and technology appeared to conflict with the common primary practice of planning across subject boundaries making it unlikely that a simple resolution could be obtained.

The fate of subsequent RDG reports, on Expressive Arts (SOED February 1991; SOED June 1992) and, more particularly, that on Environmental Studies (SOED December 1991; March 1993), showed that a consensus on what constitutes a coherent curriculum or what is meant by 'good practice' in Scottish education is not easily achieved. A combination of pressures might be argued to have contributed to this problem of consensus-seeking. For example, the composite nature of these reports, taking in a range of more or less discrete subject elements, and lacking an agreed view on the nature of the curriculum structure into which they were meant to fit, made consensus difficult to achieve. Also, and related to this problem, the different ideologies of both primary and secondary teachers involved in the work of the RDGs (or making responses during the consultation period) made consensus problematic. By comparison the work of the RDGs on Language and Mathematics appeared to have been almost straightforward.

These problems related to consensus-seeking continued elsewhere. The work of the RDG concerned, originally, with Religious, Moral and Social Education became fragmented, with an eventual split into Religious and Moral Education (SOED May 1991; SOED November 1992) and Personal and Social Development (SOED June 1992; SOED June 1993).

Concerns about many issues which were not the exclusive remit of one or other RDG resulted in the setting-up of RDG 6 with a remit to deal with these issues in the context of 'Developing the Whole Curriculum 5–14'. The temptation to offload a range of troublesome problems from the individual RDGs onto the liferaft of RDG 6 appeared to have proved irresistible with the liferaft eventually being swamped and sunk almost without trace. The publication of even draft guidelines on cross-curricular matters has been indefinitely delayed.

The development of guidance on Assessment 5–14 (SOED September 1990; SOED October 1991), met with more accord, partly perhaps because the Assessment Group published associated detailed Staff Development materials at the same time. The advice, however, on Reporting 5–14 (SOED August 1991) with a revised pupil report format met with extended difficulties concerning the details of implementation of the recommendations, the new Education 5–14 Primary Report Pads taking until 1993 to be published.

It is not surprising that the revision or, perhaps more accurately, codification of the entire curriculum for nine years of compulsory schooling should have caused problems. The tensions that always exist between central control of the curriculum and professional autonomy of teachers were thrown into sharp relief in the development of the National Guidelines. It might, nevertheless, be worth asking the retrospective question as to whether the problems encountered in achieving consensus were entirely inevitable.

Consensus seeking – the Environmental Studies Problem

The difficulties in achieving consensus were perhaps at their sharpest in relation to Environmental Studies and it may be useful to look at some of the problems which surrounded this area of the curriculum. Most of the problems arise from fundamental and continuing disagreements within the profession on what constitutes an appropriate curriculum in this area within primary education, how this should be organised and how primary practice should relate to practice in secondary schools.

Since official views on this issue were also strong, the Environmental Studies 5–14 guidelines became a prime candidate for conflict. The tension between the overt consultative style and the covert centralist style of the 5–14 Programme is most apparent in the Ministerial statements which accompanied the publication of draft guidelines in the form of a Foreword. The views expressed ranged from the welcome given to certain aspects of the guidance e.g. music and team games in the RDG 4 Expressive Arts report (SOED February 1991) to a call for more explicit recognition of Christianity as the basis for the RE curriculum (SOED May 1991).

The Foreword to the RDG 3 consultation report on Environmental Studies 5–14 (SOED December 1991) is perhaps the most interesting in that, as well as commenting on the content of the guidelines, the opportunity was taken by the Minister to make a much wider-ranging statement on the whole structure and conception of the primary curriculum.

Assumptions, which could be said to underlie existing 'good primary practice', were called into question, in particular where the practice had been to emphasise inter-relationships between elements of knowledge and understanding in the curriculum through thematic or topic work. The view was firmly expressed that there should have been

> stronger recognition ... that individual subject areas such as history and geography ... should figure distinctively in pupils' experience in the later stages of primary schools

and the suggestion made that

> ... at these stages, as at others, attainment targets might usefully be defined in subject terms (ibid.).

5–14: FRAMEWORK AND CONTEXT

and that

> ... subject based study should be more prominent in pupils' experience in the later years of primary education ...

and that

> ... the time has come to ask whether (integrated topic studies) remains the best approach at the later stages of primary school (ibid.).

Acknowledgement was given of the benefits of topic studies in developing 'investigative and reporting skills and inventiveness, and also motivation' but the Foreword asserted that 'recent research' (unacknowledged and unquoted) questioned whether topic studies guaranteed the progression of pupils' learning.

Most interesting of all, the Foreword was used as the place in which a key element of primary practice was called into question, namely the generalist training and qualification of the primary teacher.

> I believe it must also be for question whether schools should be making better use of some form of specialism in the upper primary school, to meet the increasing diversity in the curriculum and the demands it makes on primary teachers. I do not have in mind any large scale extension of the secondary school specialist teaching to primary schools, but there may be merit in arrangements whereby each teacher covered fewer subjects with more in-depth knowledge and expertise. A development of this kind would provide a bridge between the one teacher approach at the infant stages, which has manifest benefits there, and the transition to secondary school and exposure to a much larger number of teachers (ibid., Foreward, iii).

It is interesting that this was the first statement within the 5–14 Curriculum and Assessment Programme that explicitly called into question what had been accepted primary practice in both the organisation of the primary curriculum and, consequently, in the training and qualifications of teachers for the primary school. It is perhaps not surprising, given the response five years earlier of the SOED to the 10–14 Report, that the significant criticisms that had been made in evidence to the CCC's 10–14 Programme regarding the negative effects of the large number of teachers experienced by pupils in S1 and S2 are ignored. The changes to the organisation and management of primary education in the later years which were implied by the latter part of the statement would have far reaching and significant implications for teacher education and schools. It is extraordinary that such a suggestion should be made in a foreword to a draft RDG document rather than in a fully developed consultative paper.

The associated suggestion, that the self-evidently best way to organise the 5–14 experience is that there should be a division in how the primary school curriculum is organised, with integrated topic studies in infant and discrete subjects in upper primary, is unsupported by argument and remains at the level of assertion. There is a place for public debate on an issue as critical as this which had remained unresolved since the Primary Memorandum's statement that

> more systematic subject studies' would begin around P5 but that 'this (did) not imply that there should be total separation into subjects at these stages (SED, 1965: p. 132).

It is an issue which has long been recognised as a key in thinking about children and how they learn and also in achieving some resolution of the issue of continuity between primary and secondary schools and as such it might have been expected to have been addressed by the document launching the 5–14 Programme, *The Balance of the Primary Curriculum: SOED Working Paper No. 1* (SOED) 1989). That document made no attempt to do so nor has its final version. *The Structure and Balance of the Curriculum 5–14* (SOED June 1993).

The final National Guidelines on Environmental Studies also take no clear stance on the issue in giving what appears to be only lukewarm support to topic/thematic work and leaving the responsibility with the teacher to deliver the required outcomes:

> Studies presented in the context of an integrated topic or theme can be used to cover a number of attainment outcomes and strands. Much stimulating and imaginative work in Environmental Studies arises when teachers bring together the various components of the curriculum in ways which enable the knowledge and skills elements of each to enhance and extend pupils' experiences in the others. This integrated topic approach is particularly prevalent in primary schools, especially at the earlier stages, and will no doubt continue to prove popular with teachers as they prepare programmes of study. Despite its many advantages, however, such an approach requires very careful planning if pupils are to emerge from the process with a firm understanding of the relevant attainment outcomes (SOED March 1993, p. 72).

The complexity of topic studies or thematic work has never been in doubt. Arguably what has been lacking is a concerted effort to improve teachers' abilities to handle this form of curriculum organisation. One of the final acts of the CCC's Committee on Primary Education (COPE), before its demise in the restructuring of the CCC which paved the way for the 5–14 developments, had been to publish *Some Aspects of Thematic Work* (SCDS, Edinburgh 1987) as a starter paper designed to engage the profession in a debate about the nature of thematic work within the overall curriculum of the primary school but also intended as the launching pad for a programme of support for teachers. The SOED's decision to dispense with a national Committee on Primary Education, as a prelude to the start of the national 5–14 Programme, ensured that the debate was never started within the context of COPE. More significantly however, the debate does not appear to have been addressed within the context of the 5–14 Programme and teachers are left wondering whether or not a thematic approach to learning and teaching is entirely acceptable outside the early stages of the primary school. Consensus about a major area of the 5–14 curriculum is therefore far from having been achieved leaving the RDG responsible for Environmental Studies prey to the conflicting ideologies of those within the Group, whether from primary or secondary background, from school, College or SOED.

The 5–14 Programme's model of change

Added to these difficulties of achieving consensus on the content of the national guidance are problems with the model of curriculum change that has been employed. Reconciling the SOED's apparent commitment to participation and democracy (Hartley in Hartley and Rodger 1990) and the equally apparent actual desire of SOED to increase the amount of central control over the school curriculum is not easy and this has resulted in tensions which were entirely to be expected, given the fate of many previous 'centre-periphery' curriculum development initiatives. The 5–14 Programme has been marked by the speed at which the draft documentation has been produced in response to tightly imposed SOED deadlines and the limited periods of consultation which have preceded the publication of final documentation. In most cases RDGs were expected to 'deliver' within one year and the overall programme has taken only seven years to reach its current stage. This efficiency will, no doubt, be applauded in the same circles that lamented the lack of speed of previous educational reforms

> A former minister, the late Sir Alex Fletcher, used to contrast the difference between industry and education, for both of which he was responsible. In industry decisions were quickly

made. In education a minister had to wait upon interminable delegations of interest groups. Mr Forsyth was less patient than Mr Fletcher. He paid little heed to the sensitivities of interest groups, especially those representing teachers (Pickard in Rodger and Hartley 1990:60).

The speed of production of the documentation is, however, only one element in the complex process of implementing educational change. A much more significant element has proved to be the 'sensitivities of interest groups' referred to by Pickard, in particular those of practising teachers. The seven years which have elapsed between the launch of the 5–14 Programme and the publication of its final guidelines have seen a much greater concern being expressed over the increase in teacher workload, which has been caused, in many teachers' views, by the 5–14 Programme. A survey of primary and secondary teachers carried out by the Confederation of Scottish Local Authorities (COSLA) reports that

> It was clear that teachers considered that they were now expected to undertake an increased amount of curriculum development and other development work which they believe is the product of policy decisions by central and local government. Although developments such as the 5–14 initiative seem to command widespread support, teachers believe that there has been no thought given to the amount of development work expected of them in relation to such initiatives (TESS 21 January 1994)

In a more conciliatory climate than had existed at the launch of the 5–14 Programme, the SOED, through HM Inspectors of Schools rather than through the SCCC, published *5–14: A Practical Guide for teachers in primary and secondary schools* (SOED January 1994). The final publication in the 5–14 Programme was intended

> ... to provide advice to headteachers and teachers on implementing 5–14 and to assist consideration of its implications for teachers and pupils in the classroom (SOED 1994 p. iii).

The overall message of 'A Practical Guide' is intended to be reassuring to teachers, now recognised as hard pressed. The plain speaking, almost 'back-to-basics' style delivers the message that there is no need for complicated school policies, that planning need not be too complex, and that most classroom learning and teaching can be managed with no more than three groups. The complex relationship between the ideology of a structured programme of curriculum and assessment that the 5–14 Programme represents and that of child-centred learning is dealt with in two sentences:

> If the starting point is the pupil, how does 5–14 affect the concept of 'child-centred' learning? Child centred learning is about the teacher planning, teaching and assessing in a way that takes into account the previous experience, abilities and potential of each pupil (SOED 1994, p. 18).

It is difficult to avoid being left with the impression that 'A Practical Guide', in its attempts to play down the workload issue, diminishes the status of teachers as professionals, capable of dealing with complex professional issues.

The speed of development and the subsequent nervousness about the implications of the implementation of 5–14 has meant that what is probably the most important educational development of the last 25 years has been launched without any significant debate on the *rationale* that should underpin the developments that have emerged from it. The place for that rationale should surely have been in the working paper that preceded the detailed developments of curriculum and assessment policy and structure that formed the remits of the various RDGs. Its lack has left many teachers and other educationists unsure of the overall framework into which the separate 5–14 curricular documents fit. Although the consultative paper asserted that its proposals were

> 'founded on widely accepted principles' (SED 1987:3)

and that

> This programme will build on the advice and teaching materials already available as a result of the work of the CCC or through national projects such as the Primary Education Development Project in environmental studies (SED 1987:18)

it is not clear what these principles are or who has argued the case for them.

Does the 5–14 Programme exemplify good practice?

These issues surrounding the rationale behind the 5–14 Programme are important because they are part of a wider political and educational debate concerning the control of education and the professionality of teachers and what does or does not constitute good professional practice in schools in the last decade of the 20th century. This issue is highly complex and deserves to be treated seriously as is the case in the recent work of Robin Alexander in *Policy and Practice in Primary Education* (1992).

Alexander, one of the 'three wise men' selected to report to Kenneth Clarke on standards in English primary schools (Alexander, R.; Rose, J. and Woodhead, C., 1992), argues that

> Good primary practice, like education itself, is as much an inspiration as an achievement; but at least we can try to become clearer about what it is we aspire to, and why; and in confronting the various considerations which bear upon classroom practice we can inject a greater degree of honesty and realism into professional discourse and thereby make the gap between achievement and aspiration a diminishing one. Moreover, thus armed we may be able to counter the journalistic and political hijacking of the debate about pedagogy rather more convincingly than we have hitherto (Alexander, 1992:191).

Alexander suggests that in order to conceptualise 'good practice' it is necessary to answer a series of questions:

(i)   *conceptual*   (what is practice? what are its essential elements?);
(ii) *value*   (what practices do I, the teacher/other, most value and believe in?)
(iii) *pragmatic*   (which practices work best/do not work for me?)
(iv) *empirical*   (which practices can be shown to be most effective in promoting learning?)
(v)   *political*   (which practices do others most/least approve of?)

(Alexander, 1992:186)

In the absence of an extended public rationale for the 5–14 curriculum and pedagogy, it is now proposed to use these questions as a basis for examining the 5–14 developments and to evaluate the extent to which there is a case for regarding what has emerged as 'good practice'.

The conceptual issue

In overall *conceptual* terms it is difficult to do other than to suggest that the 5–14 programme is deficient in its basic analysis or definition of practice in the years 5–14. The lack of rationale coupled with the sweeping assertions of the original consultative paper mean that it is difficult to make a balanced judgment of the quality of the developments arising from the Programme.

Whose values?

Alexander suggests that it is in the *value* and *empirical* dimensions that we are likely to find the evidence that distinguishes 'good' practice from 'mere' practice. In other words do the 5–14 developments match the values that most teachers believe in and which can be shown to be most effective?

5–14: FRAMEWORK AND CONTEXT

The issue of the underlying values of the 5–14 Programme is taken up in chapter 9 of this volume by David Carr. It might be argued that many teachers feel that the 5–14 guidelines appear to ignore questions of value from their point of view and to emphasise predominantly a *political* definition of good practice (that which *others* most approve of). It is accepted that it is notoriously difficult to achieve a consensus among teachers on what constitutes 'good practice' and it is a danger that many practitioners will adopt Alexander's *pragmatic* definition ('it works for me') rather than consider the wider issue of why one particular approach should be used rather than another. Certainly, the 'Practical Guide' (SOED 1994) does not appear to encourage critical reflection on the 5–14 Programme, possibly in the interests of making the Programme appear simple and manageable and within a reasonable workload. Nevertheless, previous writers (e.g. Gatherer in Rodger and Hartley, 1990:77) have expressed concerns about the dangers of eroding the professionality of teachers by packaged material, systematised instructional procedures, prescribed attainment targets and tests. Yet the products of the 5–14 Programme, while highly structured, are significantly less rigid than those of the DES National Curriculum. Concerns by commentators such as Gatherer that

> ... ministers would wish there to be more than a mere framework for primary schools: they want prescription of content of the kind imposed upon English schools (ibid., 76).

could yet be borne out. However, at the present time the broad guidance contained under Programmes of Study in the 5–14 documentation leaves considerable freedom to the school and the teacher to select and plan their particular approach to content.

A useful test of the degree of prescription is perhaps to be found in the final Environmental Studies 5–14 guidelines (SOED March 1993). The approach adopted in the draft Environmental Studies guidelines (SOED December 1991) of proposing a set of 'design criteria' ran into difficulties:

> I believe therefore that the environmental studies framework described in this report may need to be supported by more detailed advice, setting out in more precise terms for each subject the elements of knowledge and understanding with which children should be familiar (ibid., Foreword, p. ii).

In the final version of the guidelines, the KEY FEATURES for each of the 'strands', (science, social subjects, technology, health education and information technology), set out a statement of content and contexts broken down into the three broad stages P1–3, P4–6 and P7–S2. The compromise between prescription and openness is very evident in these sections and may be the cause for continuing disagreement about the validity of this particular set of curricular guidance. The Environmental Studies guidelines do appear to provide significantly more prescription than elsewhere in the 5–14 guidance yet there is also significant room for individual schools to plan programmes that meet the requirements of their own specific context making it difficult to conclude that there is a high degree of centralised prescription.

Will the 5–14 Guidelines make learning better?

The final set of questions that might be applied to the 5–14 Programme are the *empirical* questions (Alexander 1992) that focus on the need for evidence that one sort of practice will promote learning more effectively than another. It is in the question of evidence and how that evidence might be obtained that the most controversial aspects of the 5–14 Programme might be found. In both primary education and the early years of secondary education the lack of systematic testing, through a set of national external examinations has led over the last twenty years to allegations from politicians and the press about lack of rigour, falling standards and lack of quality, particularly in relation to primary education. The assessment arm of the 5–14 Programme has been highly significant and it has, as we have seen, had a significant influence on the ways in which the curriculum has been conceptualised in the National Guidelines. This, allied with the central place given in the overall 5–14 Programme to national testing in Language and Mathematics makes it quite clear that the empirical justification of the 5–14 Programme is ultimately to be determined in the improved performance that is expected by Scottish pupils in a narrowly defined curriculum. Such a narrow definition of effectiveness may not be regarded by others as adequate.

> Some go as far as to argue that the good practice problem is resolved at a stroke by talking of 'effective' practice (or the effective teacher/effective school) instead. This is mere sleight of hand: effective in relation to what? In relation, of course to a notion of what it is to be educated. Good practice, then, is intrinsically educative as well as operationally effective. Effectiveness as a criterion existing on its own is meaningless (Alexander, 1992: 188).

The linking of National Testing with the Curriculum and Assessment Programme, dealt with by Sally Brown later in this volume, has meant that the agenda has been prejudged. Not only are the judgments on an effective curriculum to be based on two elements, namely Language and Mathematics, but, in the case of Language, only two modes are to be taken into account. If 'good practice' in empirical terms is to be based on such a narrow curriculum it would not be surprising if the schools concentrated their efforts there to the detriment of the broad curriculum which was one of the apparent aims of the 5–14 Programme.

Conclusion

The case for the Curriculum 5–14 Programme being regarded as 'good practice' therefore seems to remain 'not proven'. The major unresolved issue is consensus within the profession and within society as to what it is that we are defining as being the most appropriate basis for planning and providing education for our 5–14 year olds. After almost seven years of deliberation and with at least five years of implementation still to come, taking us to the brink of the 21st century (SOED 1994 p. 12), it is tempting to conclude that the most significant feature of the 5–14 Programme may be something it lacks – a sense of vision.

References

Alexander, R. (1992) *Policy and Practice in Primary Education.* Routledge, London.

Alexander, R.; Rose, J. and Woodhead, C. (1992) *Curriculum Organisation and Class Practice in Primary Schools.* Department of Education and Science, London.

CCC (1986) *Education 10–14 in Scotland* Scottish Curriculum Development Service, Dundee.

Consultative Committee on the Curriculum/Committee on Primary Education (1987) *Some Aspects of Thematic Work: A COPE Starter Paper* Scottish Curriculum Development Service, Edinburgh.

COPE (1983) *Primary Education in the 1980s: A Position Paper.* Scottish Curriculum Development Service, Edinburgh.

SCCC (1989) *Curriculum Design for the Secondary Stages.* Edinburgh.

SED (1965) *Primary Education in Scotland.* SED, Edinburgh.

SED (1987) *Curriculum and Assessment in Scotland: A Policy for the 1990s.* SED, Edinburgh.

SED (1989) *Curriculum and Assessment in Scotland: A Policy for the 1990s: Paper No. 1, A Working Paper: The Balance of the Primary Curriculum.* SED, Edinburgh.

SOED (March 1990) *Curriculum and Assessment in Scotland: A Policy for the 1990s: Working Paper No. 2, Report of the Review and Development Group on English Language.* SOED, Edinburgh.

SOED (May 1990) *Curriculum and Assessment in Scotland: A Policy for the 1990s: Working Paper No. 6, Report of the Review and Development Group on Mathematics.* SOED, Edinburgh.

SOED (September 1990) *Curriculum and Assessment in Scotland: A Policy for the 1990s: Working Paper No. 4, Report of the Committee on Assessment: Assessment 5–14*. SOED, Edinburgh.

SOED (February 1991) *Curriculum and Assessment in Scotland: A Policy for the 1990s: Working Paper No. 6, Report of the Review and Development Group on Expressive Arts*. SOED, Edinburgh.

SOED (May 1991) *Curriculum and Assessment in Scotland: A Policy for the 1990s: Working Paper No. 7, Report of the Review and Development Group on Religious and Moral Education 5–14*. SOED, Edinburgh.

SOED (June 1991) *Curriculum and Assessment in Scotland: National Guidelines: English Language 5–14*. SOED, Edinburgh.

SOED (August 1991) *Curriculum and Assessment in Scotland: A Policy for the 1990s: Working Paper No. 11, Report of the Committee on Reporting: Reporting 5–14*. SOED, Edinburgh.

SOED (August 1991) *Curriculum and Assessment in Scotland: National Guidelines: Assessment 5–14*. SOED, Edinburgh.

SOED (October 1991) *Curriculum and Assessment in Scotland: National Guidelines: Assessment 5–14*. SOED, Edinburgh.

SOED (December 1991) *Curriculum and Assessment in Scotland: A Policy for the 1990s: Working Paper No. 13, Report of the Review and Development Group on Environmental Studies 5–14*. SOED, Edinburgh.

SOED (June 1992) *Curriculum and Assessment in Scotland: National Guidelines: Expressive Arts 5–14*. SOED, Edinburgh.

SOED (June 1992) *Curriculum and Assessment in Scotland: A Policy for the 1990s: Working Paper No. 5, Report of the Review and Development Group on Personal and Social Development 5–14*. SOED, Edinburgh.

SOED (November 1992) *Curriculum and Assessment in Scotland: National Guidelines: Religious and Moral Education 5–14*. SOED, Edinburgh.

SOED (June 1993) *Curriculum and Assessment in Scotland: National Guidelines: The Structure and Balance of the Curriculum 5–14* SOED, Edinburgh.

SOED (June 1993) *Curriculum and Assessment in Scotland: National Guidelines: Personal and Social Development 5–14*. SOED, Edinburgh.

SOED (1994) *5–14: A Practical Guide for teachers in primary and secondary schools*. HM Inspectors of Schools, Edinburgh.

CHAPTER 2

5–14: MODES OF TEACHING

Don Skinner

Introduction

The 1987 consultation paper presented the 5–14 initiative as

a programme of clarification and definition rather than of fundamental change in teaching approaches and methods (SED, 1987:6)

In fact, it shall be argued, important changes are taking place in curriculum structure, content and process and in assessment practice – within significant implications for teaching.

The coherence and quality of the methodological discussion in the National Guidelines has been impaired by the government's failure to foresee the likely pedagogical repercussions of the course on which it had embarked, by its dominant concern for teacher accountability instead of also for teacher development, and by its attitude of 'ignoring the achievements of professional curriculum development over two decades of genuine educational progress' (Gatherer, 1990:77).

Official attention has eventually focussed on methodology and advice from the inspectorate is expected shortly (Scottish Office, 1993:2). It remains to be seen how effectively this will support the professionalism of teachers at this crossroads in Scottish educational development.

The Forsyth Paper

The consultation paper omitted methodology from its list of 'weaknesses' in Scottish education requiring action. This contrasts markedly with other contemporary analyses. Thus the HMI report on P4 and P7 stated bluntly:

> It is not only the scope of the curriculum that is an issue; it is the approach to it and in particular the teaching methods employed' (SED, 1980:49)

and no one attempted to rebut the charges: 'the weaknesses are too well known to be denied' (Stocks, 1988:86).

The 10–14 report (CCC, 1986) identified co-ordinated assumptions about teaching and learning as the key to curriculum continuity and progression. The HMI report on early secondary schooling stressed independent learning and criticised the low priority accorded to study skills as against knowledge assimilation (SED, 1986:33). The COPE paper on thematic teaching analysed the implications of ideas about learning and teaching for curriculum organisation and structure and even censured early education:

> It is a sobering thought that by the age of seven ... stimulating environments ... will have been exchanged for sedentary tablework (CCC, 1987:15)

The consultation paper's neglect of pedagogy stemmed from the New Right philosophy which informed it. New Right thinking was centrally concerned (Quick, 1988) with establishing national standards by which consumers could judge educational performance and so make choices in the educational market the government sought to develop; hence, basically, as Mr Baker put it:

> It is the end result that matters, not the means of getting there (TES, 25/9/87)

Forsyth, a No Turning Back adherent, probably concurred (Pickard, 1990:57).

But there were other reasons for neglecting pedagogy that were equally dubious on strictly educational grounds. One was the government's desire to reassure teachers and other possible critics that no radical upheaval of Scottish education was planned. When the Forsyth paper arrived on teachers' desks the profession was at breaking point over the pace of change and the prolonged teachers' dispute had created an impasse between teachers and government (Pickard, 1988). There was no advantage in presenting 5–14 as further turmoil over content and method. Hence the persistent defence that 5–14 merely codified good practice; teachers would find the content and methods very familiar (e.g. TESS, 18/6/93). Secondly, expenditure was to be contained within existing resources, with funds for curriculum definition and some exemplification of targets (SED, 1987) but not of the magnitude of Standard Grade support materials. Lastly, in England and Wales teachers had just been assured:

> How teaching is organised and the teaching approaches used will be for schools to determine ... legislation should leave full scope for professional judgment' (DES and Welsh Office, 1987:11)

However, no such statements emerged in Scotland, where policymakers had never shirked from providing central guidance on teaching methods – for example in relation to the 16–18 Action Plan (SED, 1985).

The Forsyth paper represents an inadequate approach to curriculum development, even at national level. Process, as well as content, is central to the modern conception of curriculum: ends and means intertwine; hence, any review of curriculum and assessment must address pedagogy, or court the danger of narrowing and distorting the curriculum and inhibiting innovation. A recent OECD review of curriculum reform concluded:

> Pedagogy was once easily distinguished from curriculum when the latter was a (centrally) prescribed body of subject matter and the former the teacher's freedom in communicating it ... this is no longer what education is about.

It also argued that

> pedagogy is relational or transactional; it conveys norms and values based in the belief that the teacher's role is to care for the learner's formation and that the learner is an active subject in the process of becoming self-determining. On this analysis curriculum shades into pedagogy and vice versa' (Skilbeck, 1990:36).

Besides, if curriculum and assessment are worth defining they are worth defining well. What group of educational professionals, offered the unique chance to 'review and develop' the Scottish curriculum 5–14, would interpret its remit as merely codifying current good practice, especially when that was not necessarily typical practice? Having reviewed, it would seek to develop, albeit pragmatically, acknowledging where schools were at present. Each curriculum area was in a dynamic, developmental state, full of new thinking and controversy – about the model of language, the nature of mathematical problem-solving and role of calculators, the structure of knowledge in environmental studies, generic and specific features of the expressive arts, factual knowledge as opposed to personal search in religious education. Properly addressed the issues would all have important implications for approaches to learning and teaching.

One commentator hoped the programme would offer only the most general guidance 'because we know too little about what teaching methods are effective' (Stocks, 1988:88). Was it not high time then for a major research programme, as well as a deeper theoretical review and discussion of values and techniques? Research on teaching methods was sparse in Scotland; but in England a series of studies was raising important questions about current 'good practice' (Bennett, 1992).

Hand in hand with the perfectly proper concern to define curriculum and assessment should have gone a thorough review of teaching methodology, in a way that would both inform the various working groups and take account of the issues their reviews threw up. But the opportunity was missed and the deleterious effects of the government's piecemeal approach to educational reform are apparent in the treatment of pedagogical questions in the National Guidelines.

The inadequacy of 5–14 pedagogical thinking will be even more clearly perceived if, before examining the guidelines, we briefly review the evolution of pedagogical policy in Scotland in the post-war period, beginning with the development of thinking concerning the distinctive Scottish notion of the four modes of teaching – exposition, discussion, activity and enquiry.

Modes of teaching

The 1946 report on primary education (SED, 1946) called for fresh thinking on curriculum and methods to get away from the deeply ingrained bookish tradition. The 1950 memorandum responded by advocating learning through activity, following the Hadow dictum (the curriculum 'must be thought of in terms of activity and experience') and neatly capturing the direct, experiential learning central to the activity mode, if unwisely implying that this mode alone is sufficient:

> the infant acquires speech not from instruction but through his attempts to speak; the schoolboy learns football not by conning the rules but by playing the game' (SED, 1950:22).

But the memorandum said little about discussion or enquiry, outside simple projects; and its otherwise traditional features (Osborne, 1966: 101–103) inhibited any dramatic change in Scottish primary practice.

Discussion and enquiry received more attention in the 1965 memorandum (SED, 1965), which highlighted the opportunities arising for discussion during work in various curriculum areas and encouraged investigation in mathematics and environmental studies. The memorandum's central thrust, however, was the promotion of general 'activity methods' as opposed to traditional, expository ones, the proffered rationale being the child's supposed needs for curiosity, freedom, the real and the concrete – since then the subject of much criticism by educational philosophers (Dearden, 1968, Rogers, 1993).

Another problem, not so well exposed, is the confusion between activity methods broadly conceived and the activity mode of teaching. We need to distinguish active involvement (as opposed to passive participation) in learning, whether it be through exposition, discussion, activity or enquiry, from learning through direct experience (action or experiential learning). The Memorandum's conclusion that thought itself is activity robs the term of all discriminatory value for discussing teaching methods.

The new philosophy required 'nothing short of a revolution' (Osborne, 1966: 120) and progress was slow. In 1980 HMI were still complaining loudly that 'the didactic style of teaching was adopted by most of the teachers observed' and that

> the substantial shift in emphasis in teaching method necessary to learning through activity has not taken place. 'Primary Education in Scotland' was too optimistic in its assumption that the majority of teachers would find it easy to adopt teaching methods that would achieve its aims (SED, 1980: 42–6).

By this time, in England, the Black Papers (Wright, 1977) and Bennett's research on teaching styles (Bennett, 1976) had begun to challenge Plowden's prescriptions on pedagogy, but Scotland was still bent on implementing the Memorandum methodology. By 1983, however, the debate on teaching had advanced and COPE offered a resolution, arguing that 'the study of teaching has produced no clear evidence that one mode of teaching is generally superior to another' and that it was useful to draw broad distinctions between four modes of teaching – expository, discursive, activity and enquiry. COPE viewed the professionally competent teacher as someone skilled in the use of all four modes and able to apply judgment in deploying the modes in a balanced and flexible manner (CCC, 1983: 41–48).

COPE's account of the modes was of necessity very brief. The idea was applied at the analytic stage of the SCRE research on teaching methods which found that

> Virtually all of the teachers considered (exposition) important though ... there was much variation in the extent to which if at all they assisted pupils to employ one or more of the other three modes of learning (Powell, 1985:4).

But while the term soon became common currency the notion has never been properly debated or researched. The modes concept has a considerable but unrealised potential. It provides a simple, balanced, open, flexible, and powerful approach to making sense of the variety of teaching. It cuts through the sterility of the traditional/progressive controversy and identifies approaches to teaching adequate to the wide-ranging aims and contexts of education today. Its power lies in the claim to identify four fundamentally different ways of teaching and learning and the implication that each mode demands distinctive organisation, resources and teaching skills. Unfortunately, pedagogical discussion has been dominated by the search for the one best way or the supposed general characteristics of effective teaching (Silcock, 1993b). This has inhibited proper discussion of the distinctive features of each mode and its associated skills, and, not least in the 5–14 guidelines, generated over-confident assumptions about effective deployment of the modes in practice.

There is much development work to be done on teaching modes: activity (action and experiential) learning is perhaps best conceived as a cycle of planning, doing and reflecting (Weil and McGill, 1989), for what is learned through activity depends crucially on the quality of the thinking involved. Discussion needs to be distinguished from the essentially expository question-and-answer to which it is so often reduced (Dillon, 1988, Bridges, 1979) and enquiry needs to come to terms with the debate about how far problem-solving is a general as opposed to a discipline-specific skill, and what structure for effective enquiry learning can be developed (Hennessy et al, 1993). Exposition needs modernised to match a constructivist perspective on learning (Wragg, 1993) and information technology developments (Wood, 1993). When its ideas were cast aside by the subject-oriented curriculum and assessment paper, COPE was in process of exploring many of these issues, including the organisation of learning.

Classroom Organisation

The 1946 report, addressing the need for education according to 'age, aptitude and ability' enshrined in the 1945 Act, claimed that intelligence tests

> showed the variation in intellectual capacity is much wider than was supposed and that the intelligence quotient is pretty much fixed for each individual.

Hence

> the greater importance to be attached to individual and group

work, and the recognition that whole class teaching is hardly satisfactory ....

The 1950 memorandum noted that smaller classes – a good proportion were still above 45! (SED, 1951) – made group and individual work viable and introduced the admirable principle of a 'judicious and flexible combination of individual, group and class methods'. Again, progress was slow and by 1958 a report had to point out strongly that 'class teaching and group teaching are not mutually exclusive alternatives' (SED, 1958:1).

The 1965 Memorandum likewise acknowledged that

> class, group and individual methods all have a place in the primary classroom (SED, 1965:64).

What was new in the memorandum was the emphasis on free choice activities, interest groups forming themselves for projects, and the development of an 'assignment system' for group work, which was to develop further with the advent of the integrated day and open plan schools in the 1970s.

Class teaching, however, was soon sidelined: there would be 'occasions' when the class group was the most appropriate unit – 'for example – singing, listening to music, radio, television, film, physical and religious education, poetry, a lesson or discussion on history or geography'. Officially, the balance principle was maintained, but group and individual work captured the limelight and class teaching began to be stigmatised as out of date. One apologist for the memorandum philosophy, writing in 1968, stated boldly:

> Class teaching is a relatively ineffective method and therefore seldom employed for the teaching of the basic skills

and

> the old-style class lesson is seldom a very useful pattern of instruction (Low, 1968:17–18)

Some class discussion, however, could be used: pupils 'may sing together or dance together or enjoy poetry together'. Class teaching apparently was all right for the 'frills' but ineffective for the 'basics'. It is this assumption that is now being strongly challenged in the context of 5–14.

Typical Scottish primary practice continued to differ from the recommended 'good practice', however. The 1980 report on P4 and P7 argued that although classes

> were often organised so that work in language, arts and mathematics was differentiated (by) ability ... in many classrooms, irrespective of the seating arrangements, class teaching and class activities constitute the bulk of the programme (SED, 1980:44).

The inspectors also suggested that the group and individual methods advocated in the 1965 memorandum had not solved the problem of providing appropriate work for different levels of ability.

The COPE Position Paper of 1983 emphasised the need for flexible groupings, linked to teaching intentions and contexts. Usefully linking teaching modes and class organisation, COPE argued that

> curriculum intentions are best realised through the teacher's employing a range of teaching approaches and that particular intentions should determine which mode is appropriate at a given time ... whilst it may have convenience and some social value that children sit in small groups, such groups should serve as a basic arrangement from which children can, as intentions require, regroup, engage in individual enterprises, or work as a class (CCC, 1983:47).

Another important stance taken by COPE, in marked opposition to the 1946 report, concerns the notion of ability. COPE warned:

> Particularly powerful beliefs exist about 'ability' of the child

and these beliefs have a major influence upon teaching policies, classroom organisation ... and the teacher's expectations about appropriate levels of tasks for the class and individuals (48–9).

COPE argued, a message supported by Ruthven (1986), that the concept of general ability is of very limited usefulness to teachers and hence decisions about groupings need to rely on careful assessment of pupils' actual attainments.

Clearly, there was still much to be done to develop an adequate, modern pedagogy for Scottish education. But the debate was virtually brought to a halt in 1987 with the publication of the 5–14 consultation paper.

Methodology and the guidelines

Two key principles involving balance underlie the discussion of methodology in the National Guidelines 5–14: balance among teaching modes and among class, group and individual learning. These are held to consistently from the first 5–14 working paper (SED, 1989) through Mr Forsyth's foreword to the Environmental Studies report (SOED 1991a) to the final, overarching guidelines (SOED, 1993n). The balanced approach to methodology inherent in these principles is a major strength of the 5–14 programme; major weaknesses, however, are the absence of clear criteria for determining balance, and a failure always to follow through. For example, in the guidelines for English Language (SOED, 1991b) and Expressive Arts (SOED, 1992), the four modes concept does not appear to be accepted as powerful way of thinking about teaching methodology. Moreover, the guidelines as a whole fail to address the need, identified above, for significant developments in research and thinking about modes of teaching.

A second difficulty is that, although the review group remit included offering advice on teaching methods and organisation, time pressure and the thrust of the programme gave this a very minor role. Most guidelines include a brief section on method with some examples of activities and teaching roles under Programmes of Study. These are helpful but no substitute for the principles and criteria teachers need to make effective, professional decisions about teaching modes or class organisation. Thirdly, it is remarkable that a key issue like the current controversy over the teaching of reading is not addressed more explicitly. A recent Lothian study revealed 'widespread confusion ... about the best approaches to use' (TESS, 19/11/93) which teachers are unlikely to resolve by study of the guidelines for English Language. Likewise the Mathematics guidelines (OSED, 1991c) provide too brief a discussion of class organisation to resolve issues about continuity of approach from P6 to S2, differentiation, the use of textbook series and availability of resources for practical work.

Fourthly, a shift can be detected in the Environmental Studies (SOED, 1993a) and the overarching guidelines in the role envisaged for whole class teaching as compared to guidelines published before 1992. Fifthly, the guidelines reflect a mixture of the currently popular constructivist thinking and more traditional and behaviourist assumptions about learning and teaching (Brown 1992, Bryce 1993), such inconsistency providing yet another example of difficulties stemming from the lack of a basic review of methodology.

Sixthly, the Religious and Moral Education guidelines (SOED, 1992b), in which many targets imply set knowledge acquisition while Programmes of Study suggest open discussion, active and enquiry learning, contain no section on methodology, though those on Personal and Social Development (SOED, 1993b) see methodology, especially experiential learning, as crucial. Finally, the Assessment guidelines (SOED, 1991d) advocate sharing learning aims with pupils; this would significantly change typical primary practice, bringing it into line with one of the best features of Standard Grade. Unfortunately, there is no sustained discussion of how learning can be organised to provide time for the observational and diagnostic assessment which are to be integrated into the teaching process.

Viewed as a whole the guidelines cry out for a comprehensive, co-ordinated review of teaching methodology, classroom organisation and differentiation, interesting ideas on which lie scattered among the guidelines. But by June 1993 at least, the government had finally recognised the importance of methodology in the 5–14 programme and it was clear that the comfortable assumptions of 1987 were no longer tenable.

Wider Influences

While the government tried to defend 5–14 from the charge of meekly copying developments in England (e.g. TESS, 20/11/1987), by the end of 1991 it looked as if this was exactly what was happening with regard to methodology; but instead of rushing to judgment, let us examine the evidence.

In 1991 in England the first results from the tests linked to the National Curriculum caused much concern and it was not long before ministers and the media had singled out teaching methods as the culprit. The Education Secretary, Ken Clarke, set forth his view:

> Let me be quite clear that questions about how to teach are not for the government to determine. I have no intention to seek to extend my powers in that direction. My purpose is to initiate a discussion, not to impose solutions. I want teachers to take their own decisions (Education, 6/12/91).

This was doubtless welcome news to those like Professor Wragg who, as early as 1980, had warned that the logic of national curriculum thinking might result in state directives on teaching methodology (Wragg, 1980). In 1992, Robin Alexander still thought it possible the government might go back on earlier assurances and start legislating for particular kinds of pedagogy (Alexander, 1992:179). But Mr Clarke did not need legislation; he pointed out his responsibility for teacher training as well as for national curriculum content and added:

> To discharge those responsibilities properly I believe it is right for me to consider how the curriculum should be taught and how it is best organised in our schools. Questions about how teachers teach, and the skills needed of them are central to the success of the reforms in schools (Education, 6/12/91).

Clarke presented his initiative as designed to free teachers from the Plowden philosophy which had become 'an all-embracing and dogmatic orthodoxy about how children should be taught', and to promote 'independent thought based on the realities of the classroom' and thinking about teaching method 'from the point of view of evidence, rather than simply from theory'.

The 1992 report of the 'Three Wise Men' commissioned by Mr Clarke (Alexander, Rose and Woodhead, 1992) recommended increased attention to the benefits of whole-class teaching and sustained teacher-pupil dialogue, simpler organisation of group work, higher expectations of pupils and the use of practical judgment rather than 'questionable dogmas'. The OFSTED report a year later (OFSTED, 1993) confirmed some movement in the desired direction but saw scope for further change, prompting Mr Patten to request every primary school to adopt ability grouping and more whole-class teaching (TES, 22/1/93). Here things stand while the curriculum is revised in line with the Dearing review, which advocates more curriculum discretion for teachers (TESS, 7/1/94), the OFSTED report's conclusion (TESS, 3/12/93) that that over one third of all primary school lessons are unsatisfactory implies further moves to influence teaching approaches (see also Hutchinson, 1994:139).

The first OFSTED report and Mr Patten's letter to schools raised the possibility of a similar shake-up in Scotland (TESS 22/1/93). SOED sources made it known that there was no intention to follow suit since there was 'a broad consensus about methodology in Scotland without the wide variations that have prompted John Patten to take action'. The TESS suggested that 'the political pressure to pursue such issues has lessened markedly since Mr Forsyth's departure' and reported influential Scottish conservatives as satisfied that the general approach to teaching methods, grouping and setting were 'superior to those in England'.

The timely publication of the first HMI Audit of 'Standards and Quality in Scottish Schools 1991–2' (Scottish Office 1993a) gave a mixed picture of teaching methods and standards. The early stage of 5–14 implementation made it unsurprising that mathematical problem-solving was rated unsatisfactory in 30% of schools. In '80% of the schools staff demonstrated many of the qualities of effective teaching', though too few schools had separate policies on learning and teaching and 'two-thirds of schools did not consistently challenge the most able pupils'.

Yet it was also clear – from conference comments of senior inspectors – that the aim was to steer Scottish thinking about teaching methods, as in England, towards the virtues of whole class teaching, simpler organisation of group work and direct instruction as opposed to teaching by questioning and free choice, 'discovery' approaches (TESS, 22/3/92).

The government also focussed attention on the need

for differentiation and advocated setting in S1 and S2 but explicitly rejected streaming as a solution (SOED, 1993b). Government policy in Scotland has recently favoured setting, justifying it as an extension of good upper primary practice (where there is said to be much ability grouping) into the secondary school. Such proposals have met with criticism from some quarters (TESS 12/6/92), but this looks like a minor skirmish before the real battle is joined.

Here the matter rested until, with the publication of the overarching National Guidelines on the curriculum and in response to increasing concerns among the teaching body about their workload, the minister announced his intention to provide advice through the SOED about 'simplifying the teaching process' (Scottish Office, 1993b:2).

The 'Three Wise Men's' recommendations did not just signal some politically expedient return to traditional teaching but purported to reflect a consensus about effective teaching emerging from a series of research studies, particularly those of Bennett (1976), Galton (1989), Mortimore et al (1988) and Alexander (1992). Similar research in the Scottish context was sparse but the fact that the Scottish replication (Simpson, 1990) of Bennett's differentiation study (Bennett et al, 1984) reached broadly similar conclusions, affords some justification for the Scottish inspectorate's raising of similar issues in Scotland, not least since, in the absence of a comprehensive methodological review, such questions were not emerging through the RDG reports. On the other hand, Roberts (1984) and Roberts and Cameron (1990) reported findings challenging some of Bennett's conclusions and the research base of the 'three wise men' report has not gone unchallenged (Hammersley and Scarth, 1993).

The English developments had been influenced not only by classroom research but by HMI visits (including Scottish inspectors) to observe primary education in

France, (DES, 1991) and Japan (DFE, 1992), where they were impressed by the high expectations of children from all backgrounds and quality of interaction in whole class teaching situations, reinforcing the messages from research. Uncritical transfer of educational ideas is dangerous but international comparisons of classroom practice and standards of achievement undoubtedly present a challenge to some aspects of the received good practice of Scottish primary and early secondary education. But it is also worth noting that HMI acknowledged that in France and Japan whole-class teaching failed to meet all individual needs well; more detailed comparative study would also highlight many strengths of Scottish teaching interactions and classrooms relationships which need to be conserved and strengthened as other aspects are altered (Sharpe 1992, Osborne and Broadfoot, 1992, Skillbeck, 1990. See also SOED, 1993d).

Conclusions

As was predictable, the 5–14 programme has thrown up many important pedagogical issues. The failure to undertake a full scale review of teaching methodology in 1987 and the consequently unsatisfactory treatment of methodology in the National Guidelines has left teachers without the full professional support they need to implement the new programme effectively. Four key issues have emerged: the nature and extent of national guidance on pedagogy; the research and development required to promote a balanced use of the various modes of teaching; the need to rethink the roles of class, group and individual learning; the broad challenge to pedagogy presented by the 5–14 curriculum.

The interpenetration of curriculum and pedagogy in modern education and the recognition that pedagogy involves values as well as techniques (Carr, 1994) suggests a need to extend the argument of John White (1978) and accept that, as with curriculum, broad issues of pedagogy are properly matters of national concern rather than, as traditionally (McLean, 1993: 127–9), the teacher's professional preserve. But full professional participation in the national pedagogical debate is crucial. Ironically, teaching methodology, first neglected in Scotland and in England explicitly designated an area in which government should not 'interfere', is now in Scotland to be dealt with solely by the SOED, without the involvement of any professional 'review and development' group.

Of course, over-detailed methodological guidelines will be counterproductive, inhibiting professional judgment and flexibility in varying contexts. Vague and permissive ones, however, are unlikely to generate the desired shift in methodology; the trick is to get the balance right. The National Guidelines generally lack enough detail to induce significant change and to that extent the promised, more comprehensive, SOED guidance is to be welcomed. Also needed is an initiative from the centre to promote extensive research, debate and training. Scotland has fared poorly here compared to other large-scale curriculum reform initiatives, for example in British Columbia (Grimmett, 1993).

Official endorsement of the balance of modes principle, however, makes Scotland well placed to address the varied outcomes of 5–14. Widespread early fears (e.g., TESS, 4/3/88, 13/8/88, Education, 18/9/87) that a national curriculum would inevitably mean a return to didactic teaching have not been confirmed. This is partly a result of the retreat on testing; and because the attempts by ministers like Ian Lang and Michael Forsyth to narrow teaching on calculation or history did not win the day over a reasonably balanced approach. Research in England suggests that, far from constricting pedagogy, the national curriculum is opening it up in significant ways (Vullimay and Webb, 1992, Kyriacou and Wilkins, 1993, McLure and Elliot, 1993).

The curriculum content and aims demand a much more open approach, even for expository teaching. Many outcomes and targets demand enquiry, discussion or activity and collaborative group working, to an extent that has not been properly acknowledged by critics of the programme such as McAllister (1993).

The role of whole class teaching in the primary school needs rethinking, giving it a more effective place in the teaching of language and mathematics as well as other subjects. The inspectorate are also surely right, following research and developments in England, to challenge current assumptions about what kinds of group organisation can be managed effectively. But more official attention needs to be given to the potential of collaborative group work, both as an organisational device and because it is inherent in so many 5–14 targets.

The government's claim to be able to simplify the teacher's task is interesting but it will be disastrous if 'delivery' of the National Guidelines is reduced to effective time management. What also needs to be recognised is the increasingly complex nature of the modern teaching role demanded by the system of targets and levels, emphasis on differentiation, and the sheer range and ambition of outcomes like Personal Search and Problem-solving and strands like Evaluating and Appreciating in the arts. A more complex interplay of class, group and individual activities – often within a single 'piece of teaching' – is called for, which involves a much deeper understanding of issues and principles. Silcock (1992) argues that, paradoxically, time management concerns may lead teachers to utilise collaborative groupwork which is desirable on quite other educational considerations. But recent research has shown clearly that effective collaborative work cannot just be turned on (Bennett and Dunne, 1992).

A Resurgence of effective whole class teaching will undoubtedly challenge the integrated days and assignment systems which have become firmly established in many schools and will be difficult, though not impossible, to reconcile with demands for differentiation, especially in mathematics. If the promised SOED guidance resolves these tensions this will be a considerable achievement.

In England the Plowden 'party' appears to be over (Education, 6/12/91) and a senior Scottish inspector has encouraged us 'to put the Primary Memorandum to rest' (TESS, 20/3/92). It is now surely time to do so, but only after acknowledging the seminal role 'Primary Education in Scotland' has played and reaffirming its core values (cf. Silcock, 1993a). But then it is also surely high time to abandon the fiction that the National Guidelines merely codify what most teachers were doing in 1987 and to recognise the 5–14 Development Programme as the major curriculum innovation it assuredly is. Who, reading through the guidelines, could deny the transformation 5–14 has wrought on the typical primary curriculum of 1987? A transformed pedagogy is also required. The programme makes new, complex and changing demands on teachers' professional action and for its success requires significant developments in teaching methods and classroom organisation. These are central to teachers' professionalism and therefore call for a major investment in professional support, research and debate. This has not yet materialised to the extent that is required.

REFERENCES

Alexander, R., Rose, J. and Woodhead, C. (1992) Curriculum Organisation and Classroom Practice in Primary Schools. London DES.

Alexander, R. (1992) Policy and Practice in Primary Education. London. Routledge.

Bennett, N. (1976) Teaching Styles and Pupil Progress. London. Open Books.

Bennett, N. et al (1982) The Quality of Pupil Learning Experiences. London. Erlbaum.

Bennett, N. and Dunne, E. (1992) Managing Classroom Groups. Hemel Hempstead. Simon and Schuster.

Bennett, N. (1992) 'Beyond Ruskin: recent conceptions of children's learning and implications for primary school practice' in Williams, M., Daugherty, R. and Banks, F. (eds) Continuing the Education Debate. London. Cassell.

Bridges, D. (1979) Education, Democracy and Discussion. Slough. NFER.

Brown, S. and McIntyre, D. (1993) Making Sense of Teaching. Buckingham. Open University Press.

Brown, S. (1992) 'Raising Standards: factors influencing the effectiveness of innovations' in Critical reflections on curriculum policy: The SCRE Fellowship Lectures 1992. Edinburgh. SCRE.

Bryce, T. (1993) 'Constructivism, Knowledge and National Science Targets' Scottish Educational Review, 1993, vol. 25, no. 2, 87–96.

Carr, D. (1994) 'Wise Men and Clever Tricks' Cambridge Journal of Education, vol. 24, no. 1 (in press).

CCC, COPE (1983) Primary Education in the Eighties. Dundee. CCC.

CCC (1986) Education 10–14 in Scotland. Dundee. CCC.

CCC, COPE (1987) Some Aspects of Thematic Work in Primary Schools. Dundee. CCC.

Dearden, R. (1968) The Philosophy of Primary Education. London. Routledge.

Dillon, J. (1988) Questioning and Teaching. London. Croom Helm.

DES (1991) Aspects of Primary Education in France.

DFE (1992) Teaching and Learning in the Japanese Elementary School.

DES and Welsh Office (1987) The National Curriculum 5–16: A Consultation Document. London. DES.

Galton, M. (1989) Teaching in the Primary School. London. David Fulton.

Gatherer, W. A. (1990) 'The Primary Curriculum and the Politicians' in Roger, A. and Hartley, D. 'Curriculum and Assessment in Scotland: A Policy for the 1990s'. Edinburgh. Scottish Academic Press.

Grimmett, P. P. (1993) 'Teacher research and British Columbia's curricular instructional experiment: implications for educational policy' Journal of Educational Policy, vol. 8, no. 3, 219–239.

Hammersley, M. and Scarth, J. (1993) 'Beware of wise men bearing gifts: a case study in the misuse of educational research' British Educational Research Journal, vol. 19, no. 5, 489–498.

Hennessy, S., McCormick, R. and Murchy, P. 'The myth of general problem-solving capability: design and technology as an example' Curriculum Journal, vol. 4, no. 1, 73–90.

Hutchinson, D. (1994) 'The Three Wise Men and After' in Pollard, A. and Bourne, J. (eds 1994) Teaching and Learning in the Primary School. London. Routledge.

Kyriacou, C. and Wilkins, M. 'The impact of the national curriculum on teaching methods at a secondary school' Educational Research, vol. 35, no. 3, Winter, 270–276.

Low, J. (1969) 'Primary Schools' in Nisbet, J. and Kirk, G. (eds) Scottish Education Looks Ahead. Edinburgh. Chambers.

McAllister, J. (1993) 'The ideological strands of the 5–14 educational narrative' Scottish educational review, vol. 25, no. 2, 78–86.

McLean, M. (1993) 'The politics of curriculum in European perspective' Educational Review, vol. 45, no. 2, 125–135.

Mclure, M. and Elliot, J. (1993) 'Packaging the primary curriculum: textbooks and the English National Curriculum' The Curriculum Journal, vol. 4, no. 1, 91–113.

Mortimore, P., Simmons, P., Stoll, L., Lewis, D. and Ecob, R. (1988) School Matters: The Junior Years. London. Open Books.

Osborne, G. (1966) Scottish and English Schools. London. Longmans.

Osborne, M. and Broadfoot, P. (1992) 'A lesson in progress? primary classrooms observed in England and France'. Oxford Review of Education, vol. 18, no. 1, 3–15.

Ofsted (1992) Curriculum Organisation and Classroom Practice in Primary Schools. London. DFE.

Pickard, W. (1988) 'The Political Context' Scottish Educational Review, vol. 20, no. 2, 83–86.

Pickard, W. (1990b) 'The Political Background' in Rogers, A. and Hartley, D. op. cit.

Powell, J. (1985) Ways of Teaching. Edinburgh. SCRE.

Quicke, J. (1988) 'The New Right and Education' British Journal of Educational Studies, 1988, vol. 36, no. 1, 5–20.

Roberts, A. (1984) 'Group methods? Primary teachers' differentiation policies in mathematics' Educational Review, vol. 36, no. 3, 239–248.

Roberts, A. and Cameron, P. (1990) 'Good practice in the early stages of primary education' Scottish Educational Review, vol. 22, no. 2, 95–108.

Rogers, P. (1990) 'Discovery, learning, critical thinking and the nature of knowledge' British Journal of Educational Studies, vol. 38, no. 1, February, 3–14.

Ruthven, K. (1987) 'Ability stereotyping in mathematics' Educational Studies in Mathematics, vol. 18, no. 3, 243–253.

Scottish Office (1993). Standards and Quality in Scottish Schools 1991–1992. Edinburgh. Scottish Office.

Scottish Office (1993) 'Lord James addresses teachers' workload fears over 5–14 development programme' (7/6/93).

SED (1946) Primary Education: A Report of the Advisory Council on Education in Scotland. Edinburgh. HMSO.

SED (1950) The Primary School in Scotland. Edinburgh. HMSO.

SED (1951) Education in Scotland in 1950. Edinburgh. HMSO.

SED (1958) Group teaching in Primary Schools. Edinburgh. HMSO.

SED (1965) Primary Education in Scotland. Edinburgh. HMSO.

SED (1980) Learning and Teaching in Primary 4 and Primary 7. Edinburgh. HMSO.

SED (1985) Guidelines on Learning and Teaching Approaches 16+. Edinburgh. SED.

SED (1986) Learning and Teaching in the First Two Years of the Scottish Secondary School. Edinburgh. HMSO.

SED (1987) Curriculum and assessment in Scotland: A Policy for the 90s. Edinburgh. SED.

SED (1989) Curriculum and Assessment in Scotland: A Policy for the 90s. Paper No. 1, A Working Paper: The Balance of the Primary Curriculum. Edinburgh. SED.

SOED (1991a) Curriculum and Assessment in Scotland: A Policy for the 90s. Working Paper No. 13, Environmental Studies 5–14.

SOED (1991b) Curriculum and Assessment in Scotland. National Guidelines. English Language 5–14.

SOED (1991c) Curriculum and Assessment in Scotland. National Guidelines. Mathematics 5–14.

SOED (1991d) Curriculum and Assessment in Scotland. National Guidelines. Assessment 5–14.

SOED (1992a) Curriculum and Assessment in Scotland. National Guidelines. Expressive Arts 5–14.

SOED (1992b) Curriculum and Assessment in Scotland. National Guidelines. Religious and Moral Education 5–14.

SOED (1993a) Curriculum and Assessment in Scotland. National Guidelines. Environmental Studies 5–14.

SOED (1993c) Curriculum and Assessment in Scotland. National Guidelines. Personal and Social Development 5–14.

SOED (1993c) Curriculum and Assessment in Scotland. National Guidelines. The Structure and Balance of the Curriculum 5–14.

SOED (1993d) The Education of Able Pupils P6–S2. Edinburgh. Scottish Office.

Silcock, P. (1992) 'Primary School teacher time and the National Curriculum: Managing the impossible?' British Journal of Educational Studies, vol. 40, no. 2, May 163–172.

Silcock, P. (1993a) 'Towards a New Progressivism in Primary School Education', Educational Studies, vol. 19, no. 1, 107–121.

Silcock, P. (1993b) 'Can we teach effective teaching?' Educational Review, vol. 45, no. 1, 13–19.

Simpson, M. (ed.) (1990) Differentiation in the Primary School: Classroom Perspectives. Aberdeen. Northern College.

Skilbeck, M. (1990) Curriculum Reform: An Overview of Trends. Paris. OECD, CERI.

Sharpe, K. (1992) 'Catechistic teaching style in French primary education: analysis of a grammar lesson with seven year olds' Comparative Education, vol. 28, no. 3, 249–268.

Stocks, J. (1988) 'Two Cheers for the White Paper', Scottish Educational REview' vol. 20, no. 2, 86–89.

Vulliamy, G. and Webb, R. (1993) 'Progressive education and the national curriculum: findings from a global education research project' Educational Review, vol. 45, no. 1, 21–41.

Weil, S. and McGill, I. (1989) Making Sense of Experiential Learning. Buckingham. SHRE.

White, J. (1976) 'Teacher accountability and school autonomy' in Proceedings of the Philosophy of Education Society of Great Britain, vol. 10, no. 1, 58–78.

Wood, D. (1993) The Classroom of 2015. National Commission on Education Briefing No. 20. London. Paul Hamlyn.

Wragg, E. (1980) 'State approved knowledge? Ten steps down the slippery slope' in The Core Curriculum. Exeter. University of Exeter, School of Education.

Wragg, E. (1993) 'Primary Teaching Skills'. London. Routledge.

Wright, N. (1977) Progress in Education: a review of schooling in England and Wales. London. Croom Helm.

CHAPTER 3

THEMES AND SUBJECTS

Alan Macdonald

> 'Such, such were the joys
> When we all, girls & boys,
> In our youth time were seen
> On the Ecchoing Green'
>
> (from 'The Ecchoing Green' by William Blake)

I remember very little about the seven years I spent as a child in primary school. There was my first teacher, Miss Wafer, eight feet tall, thin as a pepperoni, grey hair in a bun and stern glasses. She held up a large white card, pointed to the symbol on it and asked us to say, 'Ahhh!' At the end of my first day at school, curled up in a chair in front of a log fire with my copies of the *Dandy* and the *Beano* (which I'd been relishing and fully comprehending for many months), I had learned that I did not like Miss Wafer and that I could not read.

And then there was Miss Black and the Friday test. In Miss Black's class we sat in tiered rows in strict order of academic worth – the brightest at the back looking down upon the most stupid at the front. (In those days there were no children with learning difficulties.) For the Friday test we packed all our books and belongings away in our schoolbags which we then held tensely in our left hands. Our right arms were placed on the desk tops, poised for instant raising. We were about to move. Miss Black's testing procedure was all about social mobility and speed of response. She invariably began at the top left of the class. 'What is the feminine of "executor"? No? And you? No? No? And you? No? No? And you? No? And you? Executrix? Of course! Good! Move to the top.' All hell broke loose. Children trundling up and down, banging desks, tripping over schoolbags. By the end, six children had moved down one place. One child had moved to the top. Inspired really. Easy to administer. Individualised. Diagnostic – you knew exactly what you didn't know. Testing both mental and physical agility simultaneously. Providing each child with a clear picture of where he stood in relation to his peers. With this system of assessment it was entirely possible to move from the top of the class to the bottom and back again in the course of one test. I was, however, a consistent bottom feeder. I might idly wonder why the feminine of conductor wasn't 'conductrix'. But I would never dare to ask. And not once, indeed not until I was in my twenties, did I ever think to question the silliness and irrelevance of it all.

I suppose I must have acquired some knowledge but it never seemed to coalesce in any meaningful way and what remains today is a strange ragbag altogether – Dundee famous for jute, jam and journalism; 'Cargoes' by John Masefield; 'a smuck' being the correct collective noun for several jellyfish; a jumble of poles, pecks, bushels, rods and perches; an ability to parse, to conjugate 'amo' and to cover an entire page (neatly) with one long division sum; Black Douglas and Robert the Bruce and his spider. I could go on. But the overpowering memory is of the greyness of it all and its inexorable rhythm. The passage of time marked by regularly changing textbooks. Put them away. Take them out. Holmes Comprehensive Arithmetic. No Lumber History. Essentials of English. No Lumber Geography. Schonell Spelling. First Aid in English (for those wounded by the Essentials?). Because this was, from the start, a subject-structured curriculum. It was certainly not a child-centred one. Outside of school I had a rich life – reading voraciously, listening to and playing music, travelling abroad and fascinated by, and knowledgeable about, a whole range of things from heraldry to hedgehogs. The school was not interested. The school did not wish to know. The imaginings, knowledge, skills and experience we all brought as young children to school were to be left on the doorstep and only picked up again on the way home. A subject-structured curriculum could perhaps have been a child-centred one. I only suggest, at this point, that there was, and is, a tendency for that not to be the case.

There is nothing natural or inherently 'right' about subjects. They are convenient academic constructs. It makes eminent sense at university level to define a body of knowledge which can then be structured for the student from the relatively simple to the relatively complex. Even here the approach has its disadvantages. It tends to cloak the commonality of enquiry processes in different subject areas and to discourage the making of imaginative connections between one subject area and another. Indeed subjects are, by their very nature, inward-looking and that is frequently perceived as a virtue, as a necessary element of academic rigour and discipline. I remember at university having a Moral Philosophy essay on 'Eating People is Wrong' harshly criticised because it made reference to anthropological, sociological, psychological and culinary texts which all seemed to me to have pertinent contributions to make to the issue. Academic naivety on my part. But that determined insularity can easily continue beyond university. In his fascinating book, *Chaos, Making a New Science*,[1] James Gleick describes how the paper which originated chaos theory – of relevance to mathematicians, physicists, astronomers, geographers, biologists and, I suspect, many others – lay almost unknown in a meteorology journal for many years before its wide importance was recognised. 'Few laymen,' he writes, 'realized how tightly compartmentalized the scientific community had become, a battleship with bulkheads sealed against leaks. Biologists had enough to read without keeping up with the mathematics literature – for that matter molecular biologists had enough to teach without keeping up with population biology. Physicists had better ways to spend their time than sifting through the meteorology journals.' The sharp edges of thinking lie at the boundaries of subjects or in entirely new subject areas and a characteristic of all original thinkers is the capacity to make surprising connections and imaginative intellectual leaps. In an ever-more rapidly changing and crisis-ridden world, surely a capacity we should be urgently attempting to develop in our children.

If we track back to secondary education, where it is still the predominant model, the inherent difficulties of a subject-defined curriculum become more apparent and have been much discussed and written about and, in some measure, effectively responded to, though there is currently little sign of unanimously agreed conclusions being reached. There is the question of appropriateness of an academic model of learning to non-academic children. There is, inevitably, an increased artificiality about the way subject knowledge is diluted and hierarchically structured over a number of years and a temptation to mistake such surface structure for apparent progression and rigour. There is a similar danger of assessing those things which are most easily assessable – knowledge-content rather than process, skills and attitudes. At this level subjects can easily become petty ideologies and the badge of subject specialist some kind of status symbol – many secondary teachers would consider it demeaning to be asked to teach outside of their subject area although a Primary 7 teacher will deal with the total curriculum as a matter of course but is generally, and wholly irrationally, regarded as less of a professional because of that. There is the changing nature of the subjects themselves – at this level English is all-pervasive. And there are the acute problems of ensuring a coherence and consistency with the separate and distinctive philosophy, values, organisation, pupil expectations and teaching strategies of primary education. It is here that a subject-driven curriculum runs into the sand. This is one of the issues that 5–14 declared an intention to resolve.

When I first started teaching in the late 1960s the kind of classroom I had inhabited as a child still existed. But a revolution was under way. At the heart of it lay a greatly increased respect for children and their abilities, appetite for learning, creativity and individuality; a new understanding, given by educationalists and psychologists, of how children learn; an acceptance of the crucial relevance of that knowledge to effective teaching and an awareness that the existing structures of primary education – one teacher with a class for a year or more and potentially great flexibility and fluidity in the way learning was managed – offered scope for major development. The trigger for this development on a national rather than a local level was, of course, *The Primary Memorandum*,[2] a document which honestly embodied, as 5–14, despite its frequent protestations, certainly does not, 'good practice'. And also bore the signs of a close, creative, complex and developmental relationship between HMI, Directors of Education, Advisory Service and schools which had a great deal to do with its acceptance by the profession and Scotland's avoidance of the aberrations which accompanied parallel developments in England. It was a relationship which was to be dismantled by the present government as a prelude to 5–14.

The *Primary Memorandum* was more of a realistic document than a radical one and the journey of change it initiated was to take 15 to 20 years to arrive at any kind of completion. But I still find it remarkable that with no coercion or oppressive external badgering, no additional resources and relatively little support, but with the goodwill, collaboration, commitment and deep-seated belief in the rightness of the proposed changes of an ever-increasing number of those involved, the face of primary education was entirely changed and its distinctiveness finally asserted in a way that, even now, cannot be ignored. In terms of the effective management of change it makes an interesting comparison with the approach currently being pursued.

The Memorandum released a tremendous sense of freedom, energy and purpose. It put the child at the heart of the primary curriculum as opposed to seeing the curriculum as something into which the child had to be made to fit. It strongly asserted the benefits of active enquiry learning which allowed the child to bring his own skills, knowledge and experience to the learning task. It emphasised the importance of the sustained engagement of the child with the real world around him. It did not deny subject teaching – English and Mathematics were to remain distinct entities. And there was the entirely sensible and indeed, intelligently vague, acknowledgement that subjects would 'emerge' in the later stages of primary. But in promoting the integrated area of environmental studies it created the theatre in which some of the very best of primary education was to flourish in the form of thematic work. And to which, in my view, *Environmental Studies 5–14*[3] poses a direct and fundamental challenge.

The first primary class I ever taught was a P6/7 class. I had set up an integrated day form of organisation but didn't really know what to do with the flexibility it potentially allowed me. I decided to do a mining project because I was teaching in a mining village and hoped the children would feel a sense of involvement in their learning that up till then had been signally absent; that they would feel able to bring something of themselves to the learning situation. They didn't. And I came hard up against the realisation that these children saw school as something totally separate from their own lives. I brought in a Topic record, *The Iron Muse* – a compilation of folk songs of the Industrial Revolution – and played a few tracks to the class with little apparent response. Two girls, Linda and Hannah, asked if they could borrow the record over the weekend. I gave it to them.

And so, on a dark, wintry, Monday morning at 8.15, they appeared with smiles on their faces, stood in the middle of the empty classroom and sang one of the songs – *The Spinner's Wedding* – with sweet intensity. When the class came in they sang it again and the class was as moved as I had been. We went on to talk about the song and what we could do with it and gradually and without intention on my part a storyline developed. About a day in the lives of two families which ended in the marriage of a girl who worked in a mill and a lad who was a miner. The talk was full of – 'We could do … What if …? We'd need to know about … How could we? My father says they used to …' – and so on. The talk was excited, speculative, involved. In the end the story was quite a simple one. It began with a meagre family breakfast and talk of the hardship of their lives. There was a long walk in the darkness to the pit. They chose a piece of music by Ravel to accompany that. There was a section in the weaving shed where they became machines and had composed a tape to accompany that. There was an argument with the foreman about the girl having time off to be married. At the end was the wedding and, to my surprise, a miner's dance by some of the most recalcitrant boys in the class choreographed by themselves. It was shaped over a period of time. Much of the work we did was research into contemporary reports. It grew organically rather than being 'planned'. It was part improvised play; part dance; part anthem for a past time. And it was only ever performed once in a drab 'general purposes room' and then only for the children and myself. When it was over we were all silent at what we'd made.

Why do I tell you about this? It's certainly not at all in any way remarkable. Almost all teachers are capable of producing much richer and more challenging thematic work as a matter of course nowadays. But for me, in 1968, it was the first time I'd seen children come out from behind their desks and give wholeheartedly to the learning situation. And I acquired some simple understandings from the experience that have continuously grown in strength and certainly throughout the practice of my professional life. That methodology and a dynamic (as opposed to inert) curriculum are inextricably intertwined. That the expressive arts, if seriously treated, are powerful tools for learning across the curriculum. That working cross-curricularly is natural for children in a way that staying within subject boundaries is often not. That the more young children bring to learning the more they learn. That the ownership and retention of learning is always more likely where children can make real choices about the direction the learning takes. That effective teaching and learning with young children are often nothing to do with neat, logical, carefully structured progression but can be, on the contrary, untidy, fortuitous, creative and, indeed, risky ventures. These are understandings which inevitably collide with any bureaucratically defined curricular framework. Bureaucracies do not like mess. And the neat curricular tabulations of 5–14 documents are, whatever else, a denial of the innate complexity of learning and teaching. *English Language 5–14*[4], as a model, bears little if any relationship to how children acquire language. It does not acknowledge, for example, the long-running debate on the early teaching of reading or the very exciting work currently arising from an emergent writing approach. It will not enable teachers to teach more effectively. And the current obsessive pre-occupations with the cant and flummery of contemporary management theory – performance indicators, quality assurance, etc. – are a similar evasion of the demanding richness of the classroom.

The 1980s saw the publication of a number of case studies of splendidly diverse thematic work in primary schools of which the most widely known was probably *Mr Togs the Tailor – a context for learning*[5], an account of a lively and imaginative cross-curricular theme with a P2 class which was the very antithesis of a subject-compartmentalised approach. These case studies encouraged the identification of key characteristics of effective thematic work and the beginnings of an overdue analysis of the underlying processes. In the responses that were made to them they also highlighted two serious misconceptions about the nature of thematic work which are still with us today.

The first of these is that only a few 'specially gifted' teachers can work successfully in this way. That for the majority of 'ordinary' teachers it is not a viable approach. Aside from the question of whether anyone who, day in, day out, effectively teaches 33 children is 'ordinary', there is no evidence to support this view. What is of critical importance is the teacher's given understanding of her role. Whether teaching is perceived as a predominantly mechanical, production-line, task – 'We have done the very difficult bit and given you the curriculum. All you have to do now is identify the point the child is at on the line and perform the necessary operation.' Or whether the teacher is encouraged to see teaching as a creative, indeed artistic, activity requiring imagination, intuition and a deep sense of personal involvement.

It is true that thematic work requires a high level of broad curricular understanding, sophisticated skills in the flexible organisation and management of classroom learning and a keen awareness of the appropriateness of different teaching styles to different learning situations. And, for a time, teacher-training colleges seemed to have some difficulty in meeting those needs within the context of thematic work. That is no longer the case. The increased understanding and ability of young teachers in this area is quite marked.

A second and more damaging misconception is that the thematic approach is merely a cosmetic – something applied by the teacher to the body of required content to make it more appealing to the child; that it is simply a trick of the trade, having no inherent rationale or rigour. This is to deny the organic, exploratory nature of learning within a thematic approach and therefore the wholeness of that learning experience and therefore also the degree to which that learning is retained. I remember talking with the children who had been *Mr Tog's* class in P2, five years later when they were just about to move to secondary school. Their memory of the experience was astonishingly complete, vivid and detailed. It was as alive for them then as it had been five years earlier. About how much of school learning could one honestly make that statement? A far cry certainly from the disconnected debris remaining from my own primary schooling.

It is the starting point which is critical in any theme. Many themes have very small beginnings. My mining topic began with a folk song. Mr Togs began with the lighthearted making of a dressed cardboard figure to sit in the tailor's shop, part of an initially exclusively science topic on 'Fabrics'. Every worthwhile active learning situation, however small, carries within it the possibility of other related learning activities. The skill of the teacher lies in being aware of other naturally linked learning possibilities and giving children that awareness so that choices can be made, pathways found, small journeys begun. The movement is from inside-out. Not outside-in.

Of course you can throw your hands up in horror and say that this leaves far too much to happenstance. In practice it does not because teachers are working within the overall framework of the school curriculum and are well aware of the need for balance and progression. And are continuously taking account of the forms of understanding of different subject areas. And if at the end of nine years a child does not know the capital of Switzerland or cannot explain the process of photo-synthesis or the causes of earthquakes? That seems to me of much less importance in the world we now live in, where information can be readily accessed when required, than that the child has developed a real understanding of the learning process, its disciplines and its life-long rewards and pleasures. But it has never been a simple case of one or the other. It is a case of finding a balance between guidance and structure which is so extensive, precise and detailed as to oppress freedom and creativity in pupils and teachers; and guidance and structure which clarifies and simplifies the curriculum in ways which enable, enhance and support the teaching and learning processes.

In 1987 the Scottish Committee on Primary Education published a paper, *Some Aspects of Thematic Work*,[6] which was intended to open up debate on these and other issues. The tentative tone of the title was intentional. The area was a complex one at the heart of primary education and worthy of deep and extended discussion. Although it was generally recognised that some of the very best work in primary schools was occurring within thematic contexts there was also no argument that a great deal of thematic work was patchy, mediocre and superficial. Why was this? And how could this work be made more uniformly rigorous?

It became clear in talking with teachers, college staff and advisorate that one of the reasons was a genuine confusion about the nature of thematic work. Many class teachers and college lecturers saw it simply as a container for things given – the outside-in model. You chose your topic heading, e.g. The Sea, and then took as much as you could that could conceivably fit the overall heading from each of the subject larders. Thus, supposedly, 'covering' subject requirements. An attitude left over from previous guidance. This approach did not allow the generation of any meaningful line of development or enquiry. And, from a child's viewpoint, the learning activities did not relate to each other or have any purpose beyond their individual completion. The coherence was a purely teacher construct. A high level of superficiality and fragmentation in child learning was almost inevitable.

The paper's response to this was to emphasise the commonality of different forms of understanding and, in particular, suggest that two features, problem-solving and the nature of evidence, were kernel to all of them. It went on to identify and delineate two key processes in thematic work – the process of enquiry and the process of collaborative storymaking – and broke these down into a number of steps. Finally it provided a set of detailed criteria for choosing themes and, by implication, for planning and teaching them. In short, it made a first attempt at providing a lucid and practically-focussed rationale for class teachers which would enable and empower a much more rigorous approach.

At roughly the same time the SOED had launched a major flagship development in Environmental Studies, the Primary Education Development Project. Although its starting point was broadly similar to COPE's it took a different line of action, not least because it was, for the time, very generously funded. As well as having confused ideas about the nature of thematic work, schools had demonstrated difficulty with its planning and resourcing. PEDP worked at providing support in the field of developing whole-school policies and programmes and, most importantly, attempted to design a considerable number of substantial, cross-curricular 'packages' on various Environmental Studies topics which could be used directly by schools and would act as examplars for the school's own package development. Although there were occasional differences of opinion or emphasis between COPE and PEDP, the developments were complementary and the relationship between the two close and productive. Neither group questioned an integrated, cross-curricular approach or suggested that a return to a subject-driven curriculum would be helpful or desirable. There was a deal of optimism that genuine progress was being made in an area of school need both at a practical and theoretical level.

The optimism was mis-placed. In 1987 COPE was abruptly terminated, thus taking out one of the few genuinely cross-sector representative bodies which could have provided independent and intelligent commentary on government proposals. A move, however, entirely consistent with a calculated aim to corrupt the consultative/ collaborative model which had previously underpinned all educational change and development in Scotland. Before its demise COPE hastily published a truncated paper on thematic work. PEDP went into immediate diminuendo, fading shortly into silence, apart from a passing mention in the draft Environmental Studies 5–14 guideline as a possible source of future resource material for schools. Nothing has been heard of it since, though it may well re-appear at some point wearing a newly-cut, 5–14, pin-stripe suit.

In effect, all serious debate, on what were collectively seen as crucial issues in Scottish education, was effectively stilled for almost six years. And schools were left in limbo until the publication of *Environmental Studies 5–14* in 1993. A trifle curmudgeonly, you might therefore think, of the Minister then to suggest that schools should take up the proffered advice 'as soon as possible'. There were rumours aplenty that the delay was a result of argument between a secondary, subject-dominated view of environmental studies and the primary philosophy of child-centred education. These rumours were consistently denied. But it would be surprising indeed if that debate had not taken place. One would hope heatedly. What disconcerted was that it was an intentionally private debate and that the achievement of a broad, coherent and genuinely progressive curriculum building on existing practice seemed, from the outside, to be low on the agenda.

In *Environmental Studies 5–14* we now have the belated result of that process. Where, after all those years, does it take us?

The document is substantial – 110 pages long. Of these, nine pages are devoted to a 'Rationale'. This is not a rationale in the normal sense of a reasoned exposition taking account of alternative models and arguing for the model adopted. It ignores the difficult and crucial issues which *Some Aspects of Thematic Work* attempted to raise. Instead it makes a case for Environmental Studies (hardly required) and lists a number of unexceptionable aims. Twelve pages are given to advice on constructing Programmes of Study within a school though these significantly do not contain any exemplars of what such a school programme might look like or make any reference to the many obvious practical problems in constructing such a programme e.g. the widespread existence of composite classes. A further 68 pages give a detailed tabulated description of required content. Environmental Studies is divided into four component areas – Science (Biology + Energy and Forces + Earth and Space); Social Subjects (Geography + History + People in Society); Technology (Using Technology in Society + Using the Design Process) and Health Education. A fifth, Information Technology, focusses on computer use and would, in practice, be an integral part of the other four. Since the distinct elements of each of the four areas all have to appear within a school programme there are in effect nine subjects, each with its own sets of Strands and multiple Attainment Targets. The statement is made that 'the framework is a way of describing the curriculum and of identifying the desired outcomes of learning; it does not prescribe a particular approach to the teaching of Environmental Studies' (p. 3). Is this an honest statement? Would it be possible for a school to pursue a full-bloodedly thematic approach within the given construct? And if so, what of the related vexed question of primary/secondary interface which was one of the starting points of this whole development?

To take the last question first. 'In the early secondary years pupils' experience of Environmental Studies is likely to be largely in the context of subject teaching' (p. 10). That is clear enough. Elsewhere in the document collaboration between secondary subject departments is not precluded. But it is not required. The responsibility for ensuring smooth transition lies clearly with primaries and is to be achieved by developing an increasingly narrow subject focus. This is in itself likely to inhibit a thematic approach in upper primary and will also lay a requirement of subject specialism on upper primary teachers (and on teacher training colleges) which will be very difficult, even if it were desirable, to meet.

The document says remarkably little about a thematic approach and the beliefs, understandings and experience that underlie it. What is said is said almost condescendingly and grudgingly and hedged around with dire warnings.

'Much stimulating and imaginative work in Environmental Studies arises when teachers bring together the various components of the curriculum in ways which enable the knowledge and skills elements of each to enhance and extend pupils' experiences in the others.

This integrated topic approach is particularly prevalent in primary schools, especially at the earlier stages, and will no doubt continue to prove popular with teachers as they prepare programmes of study. Despite its many advantages, however, such an approach requires very careful planning if pupils are to emerge from the process with a firm understanding of the relevant attainment outcomes. Planning of studies, whether subject-specific or integrated, requires close attention to the outcomes to be addressed in the study and the teacher's expectations of pupils in terms of outcomes from learning at a given level' (p. 72).

Note the theme-as-cosmetic view implicit in the phrase 'prove popular with teachers'. And the rejection of any study which does not have pre-determined outcomes. Rigour is centred in content, not in process. And a line of enquiry is an artifice not a dynamic reality. And a thematic approach is, at best, condoned, certainly not supported or facilitated or enhanced. Its rationale is not engaged with.

But supposing, despite all this, a teacher still wishes to work thematically, would it be possible for her to construct a cross-curricular theme working backwards from the requirements of the document? Theoretically yes. But in practice, certainly in upper primary, the difficulties and demands are very great indeed. PEDP commissioned its thematic 'packages' from individuals, mostly in colleges, and gave them considerable time to complete them. With a few notable exceptions, the draft packages ranged from mediocre to unusable. Where is the teacher to find time and resources for such complex and detailed planning? How is her individual thematic plan to fit into a whole school programme? And how is some degree of real pupil choice, decision-making, negotiation to be built in? Some teachers mistakenly tried to replicate 'Mr Togs' within their classrooms, misunderstanding the very nature of it as a dynamic learning experience. The results were inert, devoid of creativity, excitement and challenge.

A whole school, collectively committed to thematic work, might, over a considerable period of time, construct a set of packages to 'cover' the Environmental Studies 5–14 requirements within cross-curricular contexts. But this is a massive undertaking requiring very substantial additional resourcing and external support – a fact recognised by the SOED's own Primary Education Development Project. And would the resulting programme still leave teachers enough space in the school year to meet also requirements for maths investigations, R.E. themes, extended studies of a novel as a novel, not an appendage to some other study, never mind the spontaneous response to events and excitements in the world around us? Or will schools instead, in the face of these unrealistic demands, increasingly turn to the publishers' joyfully proffered solution of subject course text-books and settle for an increasing fragmentation of the curriculum and the superficiality of learning that will inevitably bring?

In issuing *5–14: A Practical Guide*,[7] The SOED has acknowledged that difficulties in implementing 5–14 do exist. However the content of the paper makes it clear that the source of such difficulty is perceived as lying with the rank incompetence of teachers in managing learning and not in any way with the possibly inherent unmanageability of the 5–14 curriculum itself. This can be the only explanation for the nature of some of the advice given. On working with groups, for example, it says –
'You should:

identify one group at a time as the teaching group;

– give the other groups clear instructions for working on their own;
– limit the number of curriculum areas being studied in the classroom at any one time – two are probably enough; and
– give each group a turn of being the teaching group.

The profession has been right to feel deeply insulted by

the low level of this. More seriously, under the guise of offering help, the paper's advocacy of only three groups in a class (where, now, effective differentiation?); only two subject areas at a time and increased use of attainment groups and whole-class teaching promotes a model more appropriate to subject-centred teaching. It derogates the class management and organisation skills teachers have developed and the independent learning skills children are capable of acquiring and makes a crude severance between curriculum and methodology. On the tension between subjects and a cross-curricular approach it offers nothing insightful or reflective or helpful. It allows that a thematic approach is 'successful in providing contexts for learning' but does not take heed of the qualitative differences between contextualised and de-contextualised learning. It is, of course, always easier to ignore the real sources of difficulty when offering advice.

These are early days and only time will tell. But we should make no mistake that *Environmental Studies 5–14*, for all its false blandishments of being based on 'good practice', poses profound challenges to the ways of working and deep-seated beliefs of many primary teachers. Such challenges are necessary. Indeed, desirable. But this is a *fait accompli* without any meaningful public debate. It is surprising that its implications have provoked such little response from the profession. But perhaps understandable. The welter and pace of recent change, the dogma-centred nature of much of it, the absence of adequate resourcing and a continuous public belittling have eroded confidence and vision. Very changed times from when I started teaching.

There's a well-known story about a dispirited man – a teacher most likely – who goes into a Glasgow cafe one rainy Saturday morning and asks for a pie and a pot of tea. The waitress duly brings them and bangs them down on the table. 'A few kind words wouldn't go amiss,' he says.

'Don't eat the pie!' she whispers hoarsely over her shoulder.

For me, *Environmental Studies 5–14* looks increasingly like a poisoned pie. Though Miss Wafer and Miss Black may have found it to their taste. When I leaf through it I find I need to remind myself that it's supposed to be about children and the nature of their learning. And that it's written for teachers whose creativity and commitment is the one guarantee we have of the proper development of children's own creativity and commitment.

> Say the soft bird's name, but do not be surprised to see it fall
> headlong, struck skyless, into its pigeonhole-
> ***columba palumbus*** and you have it dead,
> wedged, neat, unwinged in your head.
>
> (from 'Growing, Flying, Happening' by Alastair Reid)[8]

BIBLIOGRAPHY

1. *Chaos. Making a New Science* by James Gleick (Penguin 1988).
2. *The Primary Memorandum* (HMSO 1965).
3. *Environmental Studies 5–14* (SOED 1993).
4. *English Language 5–14* (SOED 1991).
5. *Mr Togs the Tailor – a context for learning* (SCDS 1982).
6. *Some Aspects of Thematic Work* (SCDS 1987).
7. *5–14: A Practical Guide* (SOED 1994).
8. *Weathering* by Alstair Reid (Canongate 1978).

CHAPTER 4

5–14: ASSESSMENT AND TESTING

Sally Brown

The Context of Assessment 5–14

The general context in which Scottish assessment policy and practice has been developing is one which has emphasised increased national accountability in education and market competition among schools. Inevitably, the assessment environment north of the border is affected by news from England, and over the last five years that news has not been good. There has been a reported catalogue of misuse and misinterpretation of research findings on assessment and testing, arrogant and ignorant statements by politicians, broken promises on the publication of assessment data, casual dismantling of carefully and expertly developed assessment systems and gross over-simplification to support ideological stances (e.g. Black 1992; Gipps 1992 (ed.), 1993).

Scotland is, of course, different. It has, for example, no equivalent of the School Examinations and Assessment Council (SEAC) seat up in 1988 to advise on how children should be tested and examined. In consequence, there has been no parallel with the apparent debacle whereby the chief executive Peter Halsey, a former civil servant of impeccable neutrality, was replaced abruptly in 1991 by Lord Griffiths, who then ran SEAC 'much as a company director would run his board', created a 'climate of fear' and provided Kenneth Clarke (then Secretary of State for Education and Science) with 'the answers he wanted to hear' (Judd and Crequer, 1992). Scotland has also, unlike England, retained national monitoring of achievement (the AAP programme) which is an appropriate instrument for the accountability of the system as a whole, and far less contentious than the use of national tests for this purpose.

Notwithstanding the distinctiveness of the Scottish system, however, there are common features of educational reforms throughout the United Kingdom. In particular, there has been a major thrust on assessment, including formal testing determined outwith the schools, in association with the efforts to introduce a national curriculum. The Scottish version of the national curriculum is the non-statutory 5–14 programme (the focus of this collection of papers) and, as in England, much of the public debate about its introduction has centred on the assessment – the use of 'external' testing, assessment by teachers for reporting pupils' progress and assessment as an integral part of teaching to promote children's learning. National guidelines for *Assessment* and *Reporting* (SOED 1991, 1992a) have been introduced, and one of the strengths of the scheme is that it provides a framework that is to be used for *all* pupils, including those with special educational needs who have been regarded in the past as something of a separate population. I have suggested elsewhere that

> The approach is one in which entitlement to the Scottish version of the national curriculum is assumed for *all* children and anything less than that has to be justified by specific arguments. So in some cases consultation with parents may lead to non-participation in national tests or, where learning difficulties are especially severe, to individualised programmes. In general, however, adaptation and individualisation is expected to be within the curriculum/assessment framework (Brown, 1994, p 92).

I have also warned, however, that the policies which lay heavy emphasis on test results for more able children will have profound and negative effects on those with special educational needs. The effects of assessment on these and other children will depend, of course, on the balance of different purposes for which the assessment is carried out. Assessment processes per se are rarely damaging to young people; it is the anxiety engendered by the 'high stakes' of some procedures and the use to be made of the findings that is a cause for concern. It is often argued that the most fruitful and valid approach to assessment is to give the responsibility to the teacher, and that this is the least likely to provoke anxiety among pupils. It is to that issue I now turn.

Teachers' assessments

The educational arguments for putting emphasis on summative, formative or diagnostic assessment that is carried out within the classroom by teachers, rather than on 'external tests', are formidable. Such teacher assessment has the potential to encourage pupils to work throughout the year, ensure coverage of *all* the elements of the programme, enable a wider range of tasks and modes of response (especially important if those with difficulty in writing are to have recognition for what they have achieved), offer an opportunity to review the development of children's work over time, support teaching methods which promote learning and avoid examination environments which are strange and a source of stress to many young people. In contrast, external tests are inevitably short (the shorter the test the less reliable it is likely to be), can assess only a sample of aspects of the curriculum (so their validity must be in question), are mostly dependent on writing skills (which are, of course, important but not exclusively so), encourage instruction in the form of drilling for tests and provide a kind of ambush for unsuspecting pupils. Most of those who expound on the glory of the terminal, unseen test are among those who have done very nicely thank you in tests – just as those who frequently refer to 'survival of the fittest' always see themselves as among the fittest.

Educational arguments for giving teachers responsibility for assessment and eschewing national tests are not enough, however. The public and the government have to be convinced that teachers' own assessments are of high quality and are, indeed, fulfilling the potential that is claimed for them. One does not have to be a member of a Conservative government to believe that education is too important a matter to be left entirely in the hands of teachers, no matter how central their role in the system.

One rather crucial thing to be remembered is that there was no golden age of assessment before 5–14. Mary Simpson and her colleagues (Simpson 1989; Simpson and Ure, 1993) have, like a variety of others south of the border (e.g. Bennett et al, 1984), found that teachers' assessment of pupils, and the matching of tasks appropriately for pupils' states of readiness, were less than satisfactory. Black et al (1989) found that while potentially useful diagnostic information was being recorded by primary teachers, there was little evidence that it was used. Informal assessments were relied upon, but seemed to encourage broad and simple notions like 'general ability' and not to alert teachers to specific attainments and individual pupils' patterns of learning. Furthermore, consideration of how to assess pupils formally, other than by traditional written tests, was rare.

If teachers' assessments are going to be the main vehicle for giving an account of what is being achieved in 5–14, and are to be seen as acceptable to the government and general public for quality assurance, then steps have to be taken (and continued) to ensure good practice. While the embedding of assessment within teaching and learning is highly desirable, its value is dependent on its quality and on shared understandings, consistency of implementation and validity of interpretation among practitioners. Almost certainly that will involve moderation, calibration, resolution of differences and continued monitoring, and teachers will be expected to accept what that means for reflection on their own practice and scrutiny of that practice by others. Existing practice does not inspire complete confidence that all this is close to being achieved. Given the findings that assessments currently display some shortcomings as a means of improving teaching and children's learning, we have to ask whether teachers are committed to change and, if so, whether they have the support they need to make that change.

It seems clear that during the 1980s the government was unconvinced that leaving assessment entirely in the hands of teachers was satisfactory. For the age groups in 5–14 (i.e. before Standard Grade in the Scottish Certificate of Education), teachers were seen as avoiding public accountability for assessment of what pupils had learned, and communication with parents about their children's achievements was regarded as sparse. Although there continued to be reference to teachers' assessments, especially in public statements by H.M. Inspectorate, the creation of a Primary Assessment Unit within the Scottish Examination Board introduced a new strand of potential external control of assessment in primary and early secondary education. Because teachers own standards were seen as too low, an outside yardstick was essential.

National Testing 5–14

The rhetoric of the assessment statements in 5–14 from the start put emphasis on assessment in the classroom, but despite promises for guidance on this, the early documents (especially SED, 1987 the original consultation paper) gave almost all their attention to testing. National tests, indeed, were the central element in the public debate for the first few years of the programme. The Scottish Office made considerable efforts over a long period to quell objections from parents, teachers and education authorities, the majority of whom were firmly opposed to the notion of national testing of children of primary school age. Notwithstanding the arguments that children were to be tested at only two stages (P4 and P7) in two areas (English language and mathematics) of the curriculum (compared with four stages and several areas of the curriculum in England), results would not be used to rank order pupils in class, there would be no central collection of results (and no league tables of schools) and no attempt would be made to combine teachers' and external test results into a single measure (as in the notorious aggregation formula for England), widespread disaffection with the principle of the testing proposals continued. The government was obliged, therefore, to bring in regulations requiring education authorities to implement testing which had been until then, and unlike England, non statutory.

Despite the regulations opposition to national testing remained firm. A substantial proportion of teachers were not prepared to carry out the process and many parents withdrew their children from the testing. The first two trials (in sessions 1990–91 and 1991–92) found only about one third of eligible pupils actually undergoing the tests. Furthermore, parents' groups became effectively organised in resistance to the programme in many parts of the country and played a major part in forcing the government's hand and supporting education authorities' reluctance to introduce the formal testing.

In November 1992 (SOED, 1992) the Scottish Office introduced the current arrangements for testing. These sharply reversed the earlier hard-nosed external testing model and replaced it with the requirement for teachers to test all pupils from P1 to S2 in reading, writing and mathematics, but only when the teachers' own assessment indicated that they had reached a new rung in the ladder of five levels of attainment (A to E) upon which each curriculum strand of the 5–14 programme is based. The external test materials are to be used for this purpose, but their new function is as a check on teachers' own assessments and a means of ensuring a common and consistent interpretation across teachers of the meaning of the different levels of attainment. The previous approach, which was akin to nailing children to some simple-minded linear scale of national achievement, seems largely to have disappeared.

As Wynne Harlen and Heather Malcolm (1994) comment:

> Public concern about national testing meant that the attention it received overshadowed the development of guidelines on assessment, which were of greater import educationally although not politically. (p 59)

In the end, however, it appeared that the government accepted the centrality of internal classroom assessment and re-focused external testing as a support for the teacher in this process. This implied a quite remarkable change in the way in which schools' accountability was construed.

The earlier formal external tests were consistent with a governmental thrust to reduce the traditional control which professionals have had over education and transfer power to parents and central government. The collection and publication of data about pupils' attainments were seen as means of sorting out the more and less effective schools; it was assumed that parents would welcome this kind of information and act upon it in true 'market' fashion. Only the undeserving and ineffective among the educationalists were expected to shrink from the ensuing competition and conflict. So what changed things? There were three particularly important broad factors that were relevant.

First, the 5–14 programme has always been 'marketed' by the government as being based on the best of existing practice and not as a radical innovation. The curriculum has been received by teachers as containing 'no surprises' (Harlen and Malcolm, 1994) and welcomed for the structure it provides within which they can work with confidence. Furthermore, there have been few misgivings about the test materials themselves (teachers had been involved in, but not in control of, their development). The testing itself, however, was something else and was the focus for fervent, active resistance on the part of teachers, local authorities and academics. The profession was accustomed to a consensual (albeit often uneasy) evolutionary model for curriculum and assessment in which HM Inspectorate played a major part. Now the HMIs were on the other side of the fence with the most senior of them explaining and defending the government's proposals. Many HMIs, however, maintained silence on testing and played a canny middle-man ('man' is used advisedly) role. What precisely their influence was on their political masters we may never know, but the fact is that national testing now looks quite different and the Inspectorate itself has so far survived more or less intact – in considerable contrast with England.

Secondly, Scottish parents did not behave as the government might have expected. Traditionally, and in comparison with England, there appears to have been a high level of parental trust of schools and distrust of anything that looked like selection of pupils by ability 'through the back door' to challenge the principle of comprehensive education. Concern about the adverse effects of the tests (many saw the use that might be made of the findings as introducing high levels of anxiety among their children) encouraged the organisation of formal groups, across political

Party lines, to protest to the government. In particular, the parental notion of quality assurance was to facilitate teachers spending their time teaching a broad and balanced curriculum rather than in narrow preparation for, and administration of, tests. They expressed confidence in teachers' ability to assess their children in ways that helped them learn, though they campaigned hard to establish better lines of communication with schools and for more information about their children's progress.

Thirdly, there were the politicians themselves. The early stages of the introduction of 5–14 were during the period in which Michael Forsyth was Minister with responsibility for education in Scotland. His unsophisticated and narrow notions of the breadth of measures needed to assess the effectiveness of education, together with a propensity to 'take on' the education authorities (controlled by other political parties), helped to engender a destructive period of conflict which did nothing to improve education in schools. His successor, Lord James Douglas-Hamilton, had a quite different approach. He endeavoured to listen to parents, talk to the professionals and be influenced by their views in an effort which seemed to endorse progress by (more) consensus. Indeed under his softer regime much more compromise and change appeared to be accomplished than was possible under the dry Conservative hardliners in his party. The debate about the kind of performance indicators against which the effectiveness of schools should be assessed was opened up in constructive ways. The resources put into the encouragement of the profession to become involved in the self-evaluation of schools and decision-making about the ways in which they would be accountable, and the provision for research on school improvement and effectiveness, were applaudable. Accountability and quality assurance are, of course, essential in education and developments in that area were sorely needed. But the criteria involved have to reflect the broad goals that modern systems must encompass and, as the Scottish Office seemed to recognise (at this time of writing), the ways in which teachers themselves think about their own role.

A constructive and collaborative approach of this kind is dependent, however, on two factors. First, the response of the education authorities; their co-operation in the future cannot be taken for granted. Secondly, there is the requirement that teachers be prepared to reflect on, challenge and develop their own practices. The next section examines the evidence that this is (or is not) happening in 5–14 assessment.

Assessment developments in schools

The first published reports from the official evaluation of the implementation of the 5–14 programme provide some information about the progress of assessment practice; more will become available in time. Even at this stage, however, we can ask about the extent to which features of the innovations, such as attainment targets and especially the assessment guidelines (SOED, 1991), have influenced teachers' thinking about what they do. We can also examine the guidelines themselves to see to what extent they provide the conditions under which we could expect teachers to be stimulated to develop their assessment practices.

In the primary sector, Harlen and Malcolm (1994) have reported that, at least in the early years of the programme, teachers were concentrating on the curriculum guidelines for English and mathematics. The ways in which they have used the 5–14 targets in their planning, however, seem not to reflect those recommended in the assessment guidelines (e.g. SOED, 1991, p. 11). There was little sense of an identification of learning outcomes related to specific targets, subsequent design of classroom activities and finally assessment of pupils against these targets. Instead, there appeared to be a commonly used approach whereby teachers decided on classroom activities (those which they normally undertook plus an effort to fill any gaps to satisfy the content of the curriculum guidelines) and then looked to see if these activities fitted one of the targets – referred to as 'a sort of post-hoc targeting' by Harlen and Malcolm.

These authors found that in January 1993 nearly one third of teachers had not read the assessment guidelines which had been sent to schools in October 1991. Of those who had read them a substantial majority thought them to be sensible and saw the recommendations as close to existing assessment practice. However, there was an odd contrast between, on the one hand, the teachers' claims that they already were engaged in the constant assessment of children's progress and, on the other hand, their complaints that the recommendations for constant assessment of progress were unrealistic. Harlen and Malcolm argue that it was the guidelines' requirements for keeping *records* of the assessments that were the cause for alarm; indeed, the few changes in assessment practice that they identified seemed to be associated either directly or indirectly with the recording process.

The evaluation in the secondary sector (Goulder et al, 1994) has reported some preliminary findings in which Principal Teachers have responded favourably to questions about the potential effectiveness of the recommendations for assessment. Once again, most believed that they were already covering the requirements through their current practice, but still saw the demands of the proposals as unmanageable, apparently because of the recordings of pupils' progress which were involved. Goulder and her colleagues have provided evidence to suggest that very little change has occurred, as yet, in assessment practice and that consideration of such matters is still seen as something for the future, just as it is in the primary schools. The evaluators conclude

> It was clear from our interview data that many subject specialist teachers were indeed confusing the guidelines on assessment with those on reporting, viewed assessment and testing as synonymous, saw the attachment of levels of attainment to their current assessment strategies as the key task for further development, and despite their obvious familiarity with the rhetoric of 'assessment as part of teaching and learning', they nevertheless planned their development of the curriculum without reference to the assessment guidelines (Goulder et al, 1994, p 78).

If the aim is to get teachers (or anyone else) to change their practice, then simply telling them to do something different is unlikely to be effective. We know that any kind of learning requires that one has to start where the learner is and to take account of how he or she makes sense of the world. The second step is to stimulate the learner to think about how to change things for the better, and the third is to provide support to facilitate such change. Finally, some kind of accountability which holds the learner responsible for making the change (or justifying a decision not to do so) maintains the dynamic of the system. To what extent does 5–14 fulfil these strategic criteria?

The programme certainly takes its starting point from where teachers are; no effort is spared to emphasise that it rests on existing good practice. The non-statutory guidelines, therefore, have been accepted by the profession, in some cases with enthusiasm. Fulfilment of the second and third steps is less clear. Although encouragement for diagnostic assessment and subsequent design of tasks appropriate for each pupil to attain the targets is encouraged, and there is an implication that teachers are not already masters of this kind of thing, the stimulus for change is little more than an exhortation and practical support for it is very hard to find. As I have argued elsewhere

> In *Assessment 5–14* ... there is a recognition that 'teachers should be aware of and should build on the previous experience and present abilities and interests of the different pupils and groups of pupils in the class' (p. 12). The advice offered, however, is to 'collect from others information about pupils' previous experience' and 'know what the pupils should know or be able to do before starting this work'. There is nothing to encourage the teachers to explore pupils' own schemata, and certainly nothing to guide them in how to do that (Brown, 1992, p. 23).

The fourth step, accountability, could be thought of as enacted in the requirements for recording and reporting. This has encountered problems. First, it has been perceived by the teachers as the *substance* of the change itself and not as an *account* of a more fundamental change in assessment practice. Secondly, recording has placed heavy demands on them engendering resistance and, rather than inspiring assessment for diagnostic and formative purposes to promote learning, it has fostered summative measures and administrative processes. Thirdly, and most importantly, recording does not reward teachers who reflect on their own practice and take initiatives; indeed, the time it takes up encourages teachers to stick with their familiar practices and conform to the bureaucratic elements of their evolving school assessment policies.

It seems, therefore, that the conditions to promote worthwhile change in classroom assessment are not in place. On the one hand, there are the teachers who feel overworked and harassed, especially by the heavy weight of documentation for 5–14. Their relief comes from the reassurance that the guidelines are based on a consensus about the best of current practice and so they can stick with what they already do, avoid change and indulge in minor complacency. An important result of this is that formative and diagnostic assessment for teaching and learning is not distinguished from summative assessment for reporting, and the latter remains dominant.

On the other hand, the programme itself offers a national curriculum to be 'delivered' and in its concern to start where teachers are, it fails to explore how things might be different. Instead of providing support for creative change, it lapses into calling teachers to account through recording measures which reinforce summative assessment. Several writers (Brown, 1992; Bryce, 1993; Fyfe and Mitchell, 1992) have pointed out the neglect in the guidelines of consideration of how children learn and of the limitations of a step-ladder structure of levels of attainment based on the average performance of pupils at different stages. The problem is that this fosters a conception of teaching as delivering a stimulus to which pupils respond by climbing the step-ladder (see Brown 1992, pp. 22–23). This implies a passive theory of learning which may reflect teachers' current thinking but is at odds with advances over the last quarter of a century in understanding about how knowledge and skills are acquired through active construction on the part of the learner. Furthermore, it profoundly affects how assessment is perceived. Brenda Denvir (1989) has put the point rather well.

> The question of whether formative and summative assessment involves the same or different activities depends on what theory of learning is espoused ... where they [children] are ... passive recipients of knowledge in a 'transmission' [delivery] model of teaching ... assessment, both summative and formative involves finding out what is known and not known. In contrast, where children are seen to be actively constructing knowledge, summative assessment will provide a resume of what is firmly established 'robust' knowledge, while formative assessment will focus, in considerably greater detail, on the areas in which the child is currently learning (p. 287).

She goes on to explain that where a constructivist approach to learning is used

> the two purposes of assessment are in direct conflict. An emphasis on summative assessment demands that children are prepared [by teachers] to perform well in assessment tasks, whether or not they have grasped the underlying ideas ... In contrast, an emphasis on formative assessment demands a teaching approach in which children's conceptions are clearly exposed, enabling the teacher to plan activities which address the real issues which confront the learner (p. 288).

Practical support for teachers in making these kinds of distinctions is not apparent in the 5–14 guidelines.

In conclusion

Assessment in the 5–14 programme has been under pressure from general education policies which have emphasised the accountability of schools and teachers and seen performance indicators as simple outside yardsticks in the form of test scores. Underlying these policies has been the belief that such scores can both tell us whether we are getting value for money in education and provide the stimulus to improve education. One effect of this has been the prominence of an 'audit' approach which places importance on the recording of assessments, and encourages management initiatives in schools to develop whole school policies for assessment and recording.

Alongside this has been an increasing acceptance on the part of central government in Scotland that it should seek a greater consensus with teachers, parents and education authorities about the way forward. As a result, external national testing has undergone substantial change and the accountability of teachers is much more focused on communication with parents and within schools rather than to the government and general public. To some extent, this has removed the threat that the emphasis in the classroom would be on improving test scores rather than on learning, and it has left teachers more free to concentrate on assessment as a support for learning.

Evidence on teachers' assessments in the classroom had suggested that there was considerable room for improvement. The 5–14 guidelines do not seem, however, to have stimulated much change in assessment practice – teachers appear to be continuing their familiar and comfortable approaches. What is new, of course, is the emphasis on recording assessments and this seems not to have been welcomed.

At least three aspects of the explanation for the general lack of change in practice are apparent. First, the SOED concentration on the point that 5–14 is simply an articulation of existing good practice in schools has resulted in relatively 'friendly' guidelines which teachers assume are already reflected in their own practice. This sense of 'familiarity breeding contempt', together with the seemingly relaxed period of implementation (ten years?), has diverted attention from fundamental innovations in assessment and re-directed efforts towards heavy administrative demands. Secondly, the 5–14 assessment is based on an example of an 'objectives' model where educational activities are selected in the light of pre-selected objectives or targets. Over the years, evidence from research on teachers' thinking (e.g. Brown and McIntyre, 1993) and from development projects has demonstrated teachers' resistance to that kind of model. If a change is to be enacted through the use of objectives, then some novel stimulus to persuade teachers to think in that way will have to be found; and that is not apparent in the 5–14 guidelines. And thirdly, the 'delivery' model offered for the curriculum with its step-ladder approach to attainment implies a model of children's learning which does nothing to encourage teachers to think in new ways about assessment to promote learning. In other words, there are few rewards or practical support in the programme which are likely to lead to teachers' enthusiastic reflections on, and reform of, their own assessment practice.

Goulder et al (1994) have argued that 'the guidelines are more fruitfully to be seen as a starting point for change and improvement, than as an end point' (p 80). Maybe so, but this has been an extraordinarily expensive way of getting everyone to the start. They go on to suggest that we have been provided with a framework for discourse among all interested parties about promoting the improvement of pupils' educational progress. That is undoubtedly true and the collection of papers which make up this book provides an example. Whether that leads to more effective approaches to assessment remains to be seen, but Scotland seems at the very least to have avoided the excesses of acrimonious debate which has characterised the reforms south of the border.

REFERENCES

Bennett, S. N., Desforges, C., Cockburn, A. & Wilkinson, B. (1984) *The Quality of Pupil Learning Experiences*, London: Lawrence Erlbaum Associates.

Black, H., Devine M. & Turner, E. (1989) *Aspects of Assessment: A Primary Perspective*, Edinburgh: SCRE (SARSU).

Black, P. (1993), The shifting scenary of the national curriculum, in Chitty, C. and Simon, B. (eds), *Education Answers Back: Critical Responses to Government Policy*, pp. 45–60, London: Lawrence and Wishart Ltd.

Brown, S. (1992) *Raising Standards: Factors Influencing the Effectiveness of Innovations*, The SCRE Fellowship Lecture published in *Critical Reflections on Curriculum Policy*, Edinburgh: SCRE.

Brown, S. (1994), The Scottish national curriculum and special educational needs, *The Curriculum Journal*, 5 (1), 83–94.

Brown, S. & McIntyre, D. (1993) *Making Sense of Teaching*, Buckingham: Open University Press.

Bryce, T. (1992) The 5–14 model: stops on the way if not how to travel, *Scottish Educational Review*, 24 (2), 105–110.

Denvir, B. (1989) Assessment purposes and learning in mathematics education, in Murphy, P. and Moon, B., *Developments in Learning and Assessment*, pp. 277–289, Sevenoaks: Hodder and Stoughton.

Fyfe, R. & Mitchell, E. (1992) *Provision for Pupils with Moderate Learning Difficulties: Implications of English Language 5–14*, Aberdeen: Northern College.

Gipps, C. (1992) (ed.) *Developing Assessment for the National Curriculum*, London: Kogan Page.

Gipps, C. (1993) The profession of educational research, *British Educational Research Journal*, 19 (1), 3–16.

Goulder, J., Simpson, M. & Tuson, J. (1994) The 5–14 development programme in Scottish secondary schools, *The Curriculum Journal*, 5 (1), 69–81.

Harlen, W. & Malcolm, H. (1994) Putting the curriculum and assessment guidelines in place in Scottish primary schools, *The Curriculum Journal*, 5 (1), 55–67.

Judd, J. & Crequer, N. (1993) The right tightens its grip on education, reproduced from the *Independent on Sunday*, 2 August 1992 in Chitty, C. and Simon, B., *Education Answers Back: Critical Responses to Government Policy*, pp. 120–125, London: Lawrence and Wishart Ltd.

Scottish Education Department (1987) *Curriculum and Assessment in Scotland: A Policy for the 1990s*, Edinburgh: SED.

Scottish Office Education Department (1991) *Assessment 5–14 (Parts 1 and 2) National Guidelines*, Edinburgh: SOED.

Scottish Office Education Department (1992a), *Reporting 5–14: Promoting Partnership, National Guidelines*, Edinburgh: SOED.

Scottish Office Education Department (1992b) *Arrangements for National Testing*, Circular 12/92, Edinburgh: SOED.

Simpson, M. (1989) *A Study of Differentiation and Learning in Schools*, Aberdeen: Northern College.

Simpson, M. & Ure, J. (1993) *What's the Difference? A Study of Differentiation in Scottish Secondary Schools*, Aberdeen: Northern College.

CHAPTER 5

5-14: A PHILOSOPHICAL CRITIQUE

David Carr

From a philosophical perspective the 5–14 initiative raises issues and questions of different, albeit related, kinds. First, there are general conceptual questions to be asked about the semantic status of the discourse of curriculum design and development preferred by 5–14; what, for example, is the precise logical character of the terminology of balance, coherence, continuity, progression and so on, and to what extent does it adequately address the problems it aspires to solve? Second, there are questions about the coherence and validity of the epistemology which, explicitly and implicitly, underpins ideas about teaching and learning in 5–14 and about its possible consequences for policies of educational assessment. Third, there are questions of a generally ethical character concerning the overall evaluative perspective of 5–14 and its implications for good, just and morally sound, as well as efficient, educational practice. Such questions lead us inevitably, of course, into the realms of social and political philosophy to raise larger ethical issues about whether or not there are, perhaps, tensions of an irreconcilable nature in the initiative between its genuine enough educational aspirations and its political provenance and impetus. In this brief chapter I will concentrate for the most part on questions of the first kind about the logic and semantics of 5–14 discourse touching lightly upon the implications of these for questions of the third, ethical, kind. In what remains, however, I shall also offer a few observations on ideas about knowledge in 5–14 – bearing in mind that considerable attention to questions of curriculum structure, teaching, learning and assessment is given at numerous other places in this volume.

First, then, what of the logical character of the curriculum discourse of 5–14? From the large incidence of imperative and optative constructions, expressing proposals, instructions, directives, invitations, undertakings, intentions and so on it is clear enough, first of all, that the main aim of 5–14 is not to understand the world but to change it; 5–14 discourse is of a predominantly *practical* rather than *theoretical* nature. This is, of course, right and proper enough; since 5–14 is, after all, a policy document it is only to be expected that its language would be practical rather than speculative, prescriptive rather than theoretical. Moreover, there is a time for sowing educational ideas and a time for reaping their harvest in educational practice; many classroom practitioners are impatient, sometimes justifiably so, with 'idle' educational speculation and endless tedious controversy and definite guidelines offering real professional help for getting on with what is undeniably a difficult practical job will doubtless be welcomed in many quarters. It is also often said, and probably more widely held, that the true test of educational speculation at the theoretical level is, in any case, how well it works in practice.

The trouble is, however, that this very way of expressing the matter does assume a rather simplistic and one-sided view of the nature of practical discourse – one which is, I believe, largely adopted by the authors of the 5–14 initiative. Evidence for this limited view is readily apparent in the predominantly imperatival tone of the original consultative document (a tone identified by a number of distinguished critics of the document on its first appearance as authoritarian and hostile to possible dissension), in its assumption that evidence from inspectorate reports and empirical research unquestionably demonstrates the need for a given form of practical action, in the frequently repeated invitation or injunction to educationalists to establish clear *definitions* of such key curriculum terms as coherence, balance and continuity – and so on.

The demand for clear definitions, which might be passed over as a point of minor significance here, is perhaps the most telling of all in this context. For, to start with, few serious philosophers since Plato and hardly any at all in the present century have regarded the search for definitions as a very promising way of addressing either conceptual, theoretical or practical problems. But the crucial point is that even if we construe the idea of establishing definitions, fairly loosely, in terms of the search for a reasonable measure of agreed usage with respect to the key terms of a given discourse, we should realise that this search is more reasonable in some places than others.

On this point, the master philosopher is undoubtedly Aristotle who, in the *Nicomachean Ethics*, offers two crucial observations of utmost relevance to present concerns. The first is that there *is* an important distinction to be drawn in the realm of rational human enquiry between theoretical or speculative forms of reason on the one hand and practical modes of deliberation on the other.[1] The second is that it is the sign of a bad education to expect of any form of rational discourse more *precision* than its subject matter allows.[2] Some kinds of human enquiry, then – primarily scientific or theoretical enquiries – Aristotle believed (probably wrongly) to be more amenable to the formulation of strict definitions than others.

But what is the relevance of these points to the discourse of education and the school curriculum? In the terms of his distinction Aristotle would almost certainly (and rightly) have regarded educational discourse as enshrining forms of practical rather than theoretical enquiry, knowledge and deliberation. But Aristotle proceeded in the *Ethics* to distinguish among forms of practical knowledge between the *moral* and the *productive*[3] and it is with regard to the former more than the latter Aristotle wished to deny that it traded in precise definitions. The latter, Aristotle's *techné*, glossed by him as 'the disposition by which we make things by the aid of a right rule'[4] has clear enough logical ties with theoretical knowledge; many productive arts and crafts can clearly be regarded as cases of the straightforward application of scientific or other causal knowledge to practical problems of an essentially technical kind. The laws of aerodynamics, for example, established on the basis of scientific observation and experiment, may be invoked to demonstrate that certain designs of flying machine are more practically feasible than others and the technical 'know how' of aeroplane construction comes down to the dispositions which enable us to build safe and reliable aircraft by the aid of right rules. It is therefore appropriate, even essential, that the degree of precision which we seek in our scientific accounts of the causal mechanical effects of wind, stress, propulsion and so on, should be reflected in our productive deliberations in the best interests of the efficient making of effective flying machines.

Unfortunately, it appears to be widely assumed in these utilitarian and instrumental times that all human problems are ultimately and exclusively susceptible of something like a technical solution and that therefore practical deliberation is *only* of this basically technological character. From this perspective, I suppose, it is hardly surprising that contemporary educational discourse has come to be profoundly influenced by such instrumentalist thinking. It is not uncommon, for example, to hear professional educationalists (who should know better) speaking unproblematically of the *application* of educational theories to practice – as though it were the primary purpose of so-called educational theory to be concerned with the framing of scientific hypotheses for their ultimate employment in the securing of uncontentious educational goals.

It requires hardly a moment's serious reflection, however, to recognise that there is not much genuine warrant for this largely technicist construal of educational discourse and that the true bearing of enquiry and deliberation on the actual practice of education is not of this straightforward instrumental kind. For my own part, for example, I certainly believe that behaviourism is a theoretical perspective which casts light on our understanding of the practice of education and that it is an important element in the education of teachers that they should have a thorough acquaintance with the various theories of learning which have been elaborated in empirical psychology during the present century. But it is the height of absurdity to suggest – as I have heard it seriously maintained – behaviourism should be taught so that students can *try it out* in the classroom. On the contrary, the point of teaching it, it is more reasonable to maintain, is so that student teachers of any real worth may come to see that it is a highly problematic and almost certainly (for a variety of reasons) *unacceptable* basis for sound educational practice. But, by the same taken, I do not engage in debates and discussions about curricular balance, coherence or continuity in order to establish precise or agreed definitions of terms but with a view to examining rationally and critically the diverse and competing reasons which have variously been given in differing circumstances for entertaining often radically different perspectives on such issues. The greater part of practical and so-called theoretical enquiry with regard to education, then, is concerned not with the direct technical solution of unproblematic educational difficulties but with a proper exploration of the problematic nature of them in ways that address complex issues of an evaluative and widely contested kind about the true nature of human flourishing.[5]

In short, it requires only a little thought to appreciate that although forms of educational and curricular discourse enshrine modes of essentially practical rather than theoretical knowledge, these are nevertheless modes of ethical or moral rather than technical or productive enquiry. As such they are – as Aristotle maintained of such forms of enquiry in general – values-driven; moral discourse in general and educational deliberation in particular cannot but help taking their starting points from essentially evaluative conceptions of human good and of what might reasonably be held to conduce to that good. This is not, by the way, to endorse a *subjectivist* view of the nature of educational controversy and disagreement or to agree with those who have held that we cannot sensibly ascribe truth or falsity to judgments and assertions of an essentially evaluative nature.[6] On the contrary, value preferences, unlike matters of personal taste, *are* rationally demonstrable or disprovable by reference to objective criteria of various sorts. It *does* mean, however, that well nigh all educational judgments and perspectives are controversial or contestable on grounds of a basically ethical kind and that therefore all those who have a legitimate interest in the proper conduct of education have a moral right to the expression of this point of view. And obviously, in relation to education, this category includes – besides professional educators – parents, prospective employers, educational administrators and, one might just as well go on to say, the tax-paying public at large or society in general. Some of those who engage publicly in educational debates and who give expression to their educational views are often doubtless wrong, dubiously motivated or even just plain silly, but so long as the possibility remains of discerning genuine disagreement between recognisably rationally held and serious points of view with respect to our understanding of certain key educational issues and terms, there can be little warrant for proceeding as though the only real problems are how to execute straightforward technical prescriptions on the basis of certain clear-cut definitions.

5-14: A PHILOSOPHICAL CRITIQUE

But, by and large, this is the way in which the rationale of 5-14 *does* proceed. It speaks as though such terms as balance, coherence, continuity, progression and so on, are *technical* terms for which we can provide satisfactory operational definitions so that, with the right technical know-how, we can then press these into the service of clear practical solutions to educational problems. One may note here that the idea that such terms as balance, coherence and so on are the precise terms of art of something called (somewhat tendentiously) 'curriculum theory' is now quite entrenched among the teaching profession of Scotland, as elsewhere. Indeed, I have actually heard 5-14 apologists defend the rather unweildy and inflated terminology of the initiative on the grounds that it *is* justified, even indispensable, in order to deal rigorously with the professionally sophisticated and highly specialized character of the issues which it addresses; in short, it is required to do a job which cannot be adequately done in the terms of ordinary pre-theoretical discourse. But this claim is not worth a moment's serious attention.

It is simply misleading to suppose that this is where the difficulties about understanding educational discourse in general and the language of the curriculum in particular are actually located; the suggestion that educational terms, like those of theoretical physics or even car maintenance, are terms of a highly specialized or esoteric branch of human enquiry which express highly precise technical concepts (which are needed to make the practice they inform more efficient and effective) is quite disingenuous. They are not technical terms but for the most part terms of ordinary pre-theoretical discourse which are, at some level, well within the conceptual grasp of all rational agents – but which are also of such an evaluative complexity as to continue to raise ethical problems at ever deeper levels of conceptual and moral analysis.

Educational discourse, then, is not a form of esoteric technical language accessible only to those of appropriate specialist training – it is something in which anyone of reasonable intelligence and a basic level of general education can engage and to which they can contribute. However, familiarity should not be mistaken for *simplicity*; the conceptual and ethical complexities of educational terms are also such as to invite – within the resources of ordinary discourse – lengthy and profound practical deliberation on a range of sophisticated evaluative perspectives in the interests of a full and proper appreciation of educational problems. But, in consequence of these observations, it is clearly fraudulent to suggest that the 5–14 terms of curriculum design are susceptible of anything like precise definition; that assumes the possibility of establishing a usage or currency upon which everyone might agree – but this is precisely what one is not entitled to expect.

It is difficult, for example, to envisage an agreed definition of the concept of *balance* (despite 5–14's apparent confidence about this) for there is widespread controversy, not only about what should be included in a 'balanced' curriculum, but also about what such a curriculum should be balanced between – knowledge and skills, the academic and the vocational, instrumental knowledge and knowledge for its own sake – and so on. The same applies to the idea of *coherence*; is it supposed to apply to the curriculum as a whole, to particular courses, to individual lessons or (inconceivably) all of these? Notions of *continuity* and *progression* are similarly indeterminate and contested. In the light of these observations, it is hardly surprising that no serious attempt to define such terms is ever actually tried in 5–14; following the initial invitation to educationalists to define them it proceeds to be largely *assumed* that there is a satisfactory degree of professional consensus with regard to their meaning.

Worse still, however, it seems not to be perceived by the authors of 5–14 that it is quite possible to offer perfectly acceptable accounts or definitions of curriculum balance and coherence according to which any educational aims and objectives derivable from them would actually be *inconsistent*; it is not hard to see how the search for a fairly uncontroversial ideal of curriculum balance might well undermine a similarly reasonable one for curriculum coherence and *vice versa*. The truth is that many distinguished curriculum philosophers and theorists, past and present, have viewed the problem of curriculum design less in terms of how to implement precisely defined notions of balance and coherence in a mutually compatible way and more in terms of how we may *decide between* the apparently competing and perhaps fundamentally irreconcilable claims that these two goals have to make on education. For example, the long standing debates between advocates of traditional and progressive education, subject and integrated curricula, have usually been understood by those on either side to be resolvable only by means of a rational decision in favour of one evaluative perspective or the other – rather than in terms of some facile definition or redefinition of terms. Thus, 5–14's general invitation to define curriculum terms which are open-textured and contestable, significantly obscures the extent to which educational issues and problems require us to take definite sides, to stand up and be counted, on questions of the greatest importance concerning controversial aspects of human flourishing.

But *now* we can see that a good deal more hangs on the question of whether the langauge of education and curriculum design is at heart technical or ethical than might have appeared at first sight; what might first have seemed a rather sterile or pedantic question of logic or semantics is now revealed to have profound implications of a social and political kind upon which the moral health and democratic destiny of a nation could depend. The trouble is that an instrumental or technicist construal of educational discourse is grist to the mill of a top-down paternalist conception of values transmission and public good. It encourages the view that educational decisions require a kind of technical expertise which is the privileged possession of only those few who are clever enough to have mastered it and who therefore must be trusted by the rest of us to exercise it responsibly in the public interest. This is more or less the view to which Plato subscribed in the *Republic* and which effectively underpinned his general proposal to press an elitist conception of knowledge into the service of a highly paternalist programme of social engineering and control.

Earlier critics of the 1987 rationale for 5–14[7] detected a distinct authoritarian or paternalist tone in the document which somewhat belied the rhetoric of professional consultation and dialogue and gave rise to suspicions of a hidden political agenda with respect to its proposals. Whilst it is always possible (on a more charitable view) to suppose that the authors of the rationale were simply misled by an error about the logic of educational discourse into construing what is at heart a form of democratic-participatory discourse, to which each and every rational and informed citizen has a basic moral right to contribute, for a form of technical discourse which gives some, the alleged experts, a right to make some of the decisions of non-experts for them – there is clearly, nevertheless, a real enough tension in the 5–14 documentation between the democratic language of consultation and the *de haut en bas* tones of political paternalism.

There is also, I believe, abundant evidence in the available 5–14 documentation for the overall account of the character of the initiative which I have been concerned to offer here and which has been echoed by others elsewhere; the paternalist-instrumentalist flavour of 5–14's general approach to matters of curriculum design and development is discernible in most aspects of the programme. Moreover, since it would be almost indecent to conclude a philosophical investigation of a curriculum initiative without some comment on epistemological matters I will end with some remarks about how 5–14's view of *knowledge* would seem to be related to the sort of considerations aired so far.

Curiously, it seems not to have been observed in any criticisms of the initiative of which I am aware, that 5–14 proceeds in the light of a most peculiar definition of knowledge. In Working Paper No. 1 which purports to set out the basic aims of primary education, as well as a basic curriculum framework for the programme, it is clearly stated that: 'In all aspects of learning the acquisition of *knowledge* is necessary to achieve *understanding*'.[8] It can hardly be overstated that, in terms of traditional epistemology, this represents a highly *eccentric* view. For, on the orthodox account (which we owe, in essentials, to Plato's *Theaetetus*) knowledge is construed in terms of three conditions which, though later philosophers have disputed their joint sufficiency,[9] have seldom been doubted as severally *necessary* for any satisfactory analysis of the notion. The first of these, which we may call the *truth* condition, is that any statement purporting to express an item of knowledge must at the very least be true. The second, which we can call the *psychological* condition, recognises that knowledge claims also ordinarily presuppose some degree of credence or acceptance of what is known on the part of the individual who knows; it is paradoxical to claim knowledge of something whilst denying that one believes it. The third condition, however, asserts that knowledge is more than just a matter of true belief; it also entails what Plato called a *logos*. This feature is sometimes construed, somewhat narrowly, as an *evidence* condition; it is not sufficient for genuine knowledge that p, that we should merely believe (correctly) p to be true – we should also have *grounds* for believing p. But, on a rather broader interpretation of *logos*, grounds can mean almost any item within a range of what philosophical logicians would call 'intensional' operators or functions – evidence, proof, explanation, justification, reason, a grasp of significance or *understanding*. In short, far from it being the case that I need to know that an *aranea diadema* is a species of *arachnida* in order to understand it, I could not reasonably claim to know it unless I first understood what it meant; in short, understanding contributes to the definition of knowledge and not, contrary to 5–14, *vice versa*.

Indeed, what could be meant by knowledge apart from or in advance of understanding?; surely only the psychological retention of true beliefs – facts or items of information – which an individual registers on the word, or retains at the will or behest, of others. Is it really possible to register facts without any understanding? It is not only possible, many educational progressives and radicals would say, but it has been the chief characteristic of conventional state education at least since the days of Gradgrind[10] and probably well before. On this view, generations of schoolchildren have been trained or drilled in mere habits of recall with respect to facts and information they did not in the least understand; they believed what was (sometimes) true – but in the absence of a proper grasp of what they believed they had nothing worth calling knowledge.

But worse is to come; for what implications can 5–14's peculiar redefinition of knowledge as a state conceived *independently* of understanding, and of understanding *in terms of* knowledge thus construed, have for any conception of the growth of understanding? It is hard to avoid the conclusion, according to such a redefinition, that understanding amounts to little more than some sort of accumulation or concatenation of (perhaps meaningless) facts. Knowingly or otherwise, then, 5–14 appears to have endorsed a crude kind of empiricist or associationist view of learning or knowledge acquisition according to which there is little more to understanding than an incremental growth of inputs from experience (broadly construed). Thus, the perverse construal of understanding in terms of so-called knowledge (but what is rather less) must lead not only to an inadequate and ultimately incoherent view of knowledge but also to the impossibility of offering any substantial account of understanding which goes beyond the idea of amassing to much possibly meaningless information.

But isn't this really just an idle philosopher's quibble – just a case of blowing an understandable mistake or slip or the pen out of all proportion for the sake of mischievousness or point-scoring? I really do not think so. I believe that what I have called a redefinition of knowledge fits very neatly – and more than just accidentally – with the observations so far made about the top-down character of the overall proposals, the general framework of outcome-focused aims and objectives in terms of which the whole 5–14 programme is set out, the assessment driven nature of the initiative and the rather superficial ideas about assessment which inform it and, above all, the crude traditionalist views about the nature of knowledge, the attacks on progressive and process models of education and the remarks about getting back to basics which have been publicly uttered by leading figures of the very same political administration which has promoted the 5–14 initiative.

No space remains for a chapter and verse substantiation of this general claim which would require a detailed examination of all the items of the 5–14 documentation which have appeared to date. It only remains to be said that I regard most of the treatments which have so far been offered of important aspects of the P1–S2 curriculum to be seriously impaired by virtue of a regrettable attempt to force much commendable professional thinking about the nature of worthwhile educational experience into the procrustean bed of a curriculum framework which is at heart ideologically motivated. An example of this, on which I have commented elsewhere,[11] is the 5–14 treatment of moral and religious education concerning which an initially absurd proposal to assign a time allocation to an area of human experience and education which cannot be so quantified, issues ultimately in a bizarrely decontextualized conception of how that experience comes to acquire human significance and an unplumbably shallow idea of what might constitute educational success with respect to it. It is, of course, entirely in vain for educational professionals having been drafted into the detailed writing of an initiative such as 5–14 to set as 'attainment targets' that children should *understand* this and appreciate the *significance* of that when it is not otherwise clear from the rationale, 'definitions' of knowledge and so on, and the way the aims and objectives have been framed, that genuine ownership of knowledge entailing a proper understanding of their human, social and political predicament is high on the agenda of our political masters – *either* for children and young people in our schools *or* for the teachers who teach them.

REFERENCES

1. Aristotle, *The Nicomachean Ethics*, translated by Sir David Ross. London: Oxford University Press, 1969. Book VI, especially section 5.
2. *Ibid.*, p. 2.
3. *Ibid.*, Book VI, sections 4 and 5.
4. *Ibid.*, Book VI, section 4.
5. I have made this point fully in my: Practical enquiry, values and the problem of educational theory. *Oxford Review of Education*, Volume 41, No. 3, 1992. See also my: Questions of competence, *British Journal of Educational Studies*, Volume 41, No. 3, 1993.
6. For a full argument for ethical and evaluative objectivism in relation to education, see my: Education and values, *British Journal of Educational Studies*, Volume 39, No. 3, 1991.
7. See, for example, the various contributors to a symposium on the 1987 rationale for 5–14 published in the *Scottish Educational Review*, Volume 20, 1988. The contribution of Dr Bill Gatherer entitled: *The Two Voices* – is of especial interest in relation to this criticism.
8. Scottish Education Department: *Curriculum and Assessment in Scotland: A Policy for the 90s*. Working Paper No. 1: *The Balance of the Primary Curriculum*, March 1989, p. 3.
9. See, for example, E. L. Gettier, Is knowledge justified true belief? in A. Phillips Griffiths (ed.) *Knowledge and Belief*. Oxford Readings in Philosophy. Oxford University Press, 1967.

10. Gradgrind, a character in Charles Dicken's novel *Hard Times*, is the archetypal model of repressive and sterile pedagogy.
11. See my: Moral and religious education 5–14. *Scottish Educational Review*, Volume 24, No. 2, 1992.

APPENDIX 1

CURRICULUM AREAS IN 5–14 DEVELOPMENT PROGRAMME

ENGLISH LANGUAGE	
ATTAINMENT OUTCOMES	**STRANDS**
Listening	Listening for information, instructions and directions Listening in groups Listening in order to respond to texts Awareness of genre (type of text) Knowledge about language
Talking	Conveying information, instructions and directions Talking in groups Talking about experiences, feelings and opinions Talking about texts Audience awareness Knowledge about language
Reading	Reading for information Reading for enjoyment Reading to reflect on the writer's ideas and craft Awareness of genre (type of text) Reading aloud Knowledge about language
Writing	Functional writing Personal writing Imaginative writing Punctuation and structure Spelling Handwriting and presentation Knowledge about language

MATHEMATICS

ATTAINMENT OUTCOMES	STRANDS
Problem-solving & enquiry	Problem-solving and enquiry
Information handling	Collect Organise Display Interpret
Number, money & measurement	Range and type of numbers Money Add and subtract Multiply and divide Round numbers Fractions, percentages and ratio Patterns and sequences Functions and equations Measure and estimate Time Perimeter, formulae, scales
Shape, position & movement	Range of shapes Position and movement Symmetry Angle

RELIGIOUS AND MORAL EDUCATION

ATTAINMENT OUTCOMES	STRANDS
Christianity	Celebrations, festivals, ceremonies and customs Sacred writings, stories and key figures Beliefs Sacred places, worship and symbols Moral values and attitudes
Other World Religions	Celebrations, festivals, ceremonies and customs Sacred writings, stories and key figures Beliefs Sacred places, worship and symbols Moral values and attitudes
Personal Search in Relation to:	The natural world Relationships and moral values Ultimate questions

PERSONAL AND SOCIAL DEVELOPMENT

OUTCOMES	CONCERNED WITH
Personal Development	Self-Awareness Self-Esteem
Social Development	Inter-personal relationships Independence and inter-dependence

ENVIRONMENTAL STUDIES

ATTAINMENT OUTCOMES	STRANDS
Science Understanding living things and the processes of life Understanding energy and forces Understanding earth and space	Knowledge and understanding Planning Collecting evidence Recording and presenting Interpreting and evaluating Developing informed attitudes
Social Subjects Understanding people and place Understanding people in the past Understanding people in society	Knowledge and understanding Planning Collecting evidence Recording and presenting Interpreting and evaluating Developing informed attitudes
Technology Understanding and using technology in society Understanding and using the design process	Knowledge and understanding Planning Collecting evidence Applying skills and presenting solutions Interpreting and evaluating Developing informed attitudes
Health Education Healthy and Safe Living	Knowledge and understanding Taking action on health
Information Technology Understanding and Using Information Technology	Knowledge and understanding Using information technology

EXPRESSIVE ARTS

ATTAINMENT OUTCOMES	STRANDS
Art & Design Using materials techniques, skills and media	Investigating visually and recording Using media Using visual elements
Expressing feelings, ideas, thoughts and solutions	Creating and designing Communicating
Evaluating & appreciating	Observing, reflecting, describing and responding
Drama Using materials techniques, skills and media	Investigating and experimenting Using movement and mime Using language
Expressing feelings, ideas, thoughts and solutions	Creating and designing Communicating and presenting
Evaluating & appreciating	Observing, listening, reflecting describing and responding
Music Using materials techniques, skills and media	Investigating: exploring sound Using the voice Using instruments
Expressing feelings, ideas, thoughts and solutions	Creating and designing Communicating and presenting
Evaluating & appreciating	Observing, listening, reflecting describing and responding
Physical Education Using materials techniques, skills and media	Investigating and developing fitness Using the body Applying skills
Expressing feelings, ideas, thoughts and solutions	Creating and designing Cooperating, sharing, communicating and competing
Evaluating & appreciating	Observing, reflecting, describing and responding

GAELIC MEDIUM

ATTAINMENT OUTCOMES	STRANDS
Listening	Listening for information, instructions and directions Listening in groups Listening in order to respond to texts Awareness of genre (type of text) Knowledge about language
Talking	Conveying information, instructions and directions Talking in groups Talking about experiences, feelings and opinions Talking about texts Audience awareness Knowledge about language
Reading	Reading for information Reading for enjoyment Reading to relect on the writer's ideas and craft Awareness of genre (type of text) Reading aloud Knowledge about language
Writing	Functional writing Personal writing Imaginative writing Punctuation and structure Spelling Handwriting and presentation Knowledge about language

GAELIC LEARNERS

ATTAINMENT OUTCOMES	STRANDS
Listening	Understand personal information Understand general information Respond to instructions and directions Respond to requests Understand expressions of feelings and opinions Understand descriptions
Talking	Convey personal information Convey general information Give instructions and directions Make requests Talk about feelings and opinions Describe
Reading	Reading for information Finding and handling information Reading aloud

LATIN	
ATTAINMENT OUTCOMES	**STRANDS**
Translating/ Interpreting Texts	Grammar Vocabulary Reference skills Conveying meaning Content explanation Personal response
Knowledge about Language	Linguistic terminology Awareness of structure Etymology
The Roman World	Gathering and presenting information Knowledge of Roman life Comparison Personal response

MODERN EUROPEAN LANGUAGES

ATTAINMENT OUTCOMES	STRANDS
Listening	Classroom language Listening to establish relationships with others Listening for information
Speaking	Classroom language Speaking to establish relationships with others Speaking on a topic Asking for support Pronunciation and intonation Knowledge about language
Reading	Reading for information Reading for enjoyment Pronunciation and the written word Using reference sources
Writing	Copying Writing from memory Continuous writing

JUVÉNILIA

Titres originaux :
Love and Freindship
The Three Sisters
Jack and Alice

Traduit de l'anglais par Laura Bourgeois

© Charleston, une marque des éditions Leduc.s, 2017
29 boulevard Raspail
75007 Paris - France
contact@editionscharleston.fr
www.editionscharleston.fr

ISBN : 978-2-36812-151-1

Maquette : Patrick Leleux PAO

Pour suivre notre actualité, rejoignez-nous sur la page Facebook : www.facebook.com/Editions.Charleston et sur Twitter @LillyCharleston

Jane Austen

JUVÉNILIA

Amour et Amitié – Les Trois Sœurs – Jack et Alice

Traduit de l'anglais par Laura Bourgeois

Amour et amitié

Un roman épistolaire

« Trompée en amitié et trahie en amour. »
À Madame la Comtesse de Feuillide,
ce roman est dédié en reconnaissance
par son humble servante,

L'Auteur.

Lettre I

De Isabel à Laura

Combien de fois, en réponse à mes instances renouvelées de faire à ma fille le récit de vos malheurs et aventures, m'avez-vous dit « Non, chère amie, jamais je n'accéderai à votre requête tant que me guettera le péril de connaître à nouveau de telles souffrances. »

Assurément, ce temps est désormais révolu puisque vous avez aujourd'hui cinquante-cinq ans. Si une femme peut un jour se considérer à l'abri de la persévérance téméraire d'amants déplaisants et des cruelles persécutions de pères obstinés, ce ne peut être qu'à cet âge de la vie.

Isabel.

Lettre II

Laura à Isabel

Bien que je ne puisse vous donner raison et supposer que jamais plus je ne me retrouverai exposée aux malheurs injustes dont j'ai souffert, et afin d'éviter que l'on m'impute un caractère mauvais et implacable, j'entends satisfaire la curiosité de votre fille. Puisse la force d'âme avec laquelle j'ai enduré les nombreuses afflictions de ma vie passée lui donner une leçon utile pour affronter celles qui pourraient se dresser sur son chemin.

Laura.

Lettre III

Laura à Marianne

Puisque vous êtes la fille de mon amie la plus chère, vous méritez d'entendre ma triste histoire, celle que votre mère m'a tant priée de vous conter.

D'un père irlandais de naissance, installé au pays de Galles, et d'une mère enfant naturelle d'un pair d'Écosse et d'une danseuse d'opéra italienne, je naquis en Espagne et reçus mon instruction dans un couvent français.

L'année de mes dix-huit ans, mes parents me rappelèrent au domaine paternel du pays de Galles. Notre manoir était situé dans une des régions les plus romantiques de la vallée de l'Usk. Si mes charmes sont désormais considérablement amoindris et marqués par les malheurs que j'ai endurés, je fus jadis belle. Pourtant, les grâces de ma personne n'étaient pas les premières de mes perfections. De chaque qualité imputée à mon sexe, j'étais maîtresse. Au couvent, mes progrès avaient toujours surpassé mon instruction, le nombre de mes acquis était remarquable pour mon âge, et je dépassais mes maîtres.

Mon esprit était doté de toutes les vertus imaginables ; aucune qualité, aucun noble sentiment ne me faisait défaut.

Une sensibilité rendue trop vulnérable à l'affliction de mes amis, parents, et plus encore aux miennes, était mon seul défaut, si l'on peut le nommer ainsi. Hélas ! Qu'en reste-t-il à présent ! Si mes propres malheurs ne m'affectent pas moins que jadis, je suis désormais insensible à ceux des autres. Mes talents aussi commencent à se faner – je ne puis plus chanter si bien, ni danser avec autant de grâce – et j'ai tout à fait oublié le *Menuet de la Cour*.

Adieu,
Laura.

Lettre IV

Laura à Marianne

Notre voisinage n'était que peu de chose, puisqu'il se limitait à votre mère. Elle vous aura peut-être déjà rapporté qu'après avoir été laissée par ses parents dans d'indigentes circonstances, elle se retira au pays de Galles pour des raisons pécuniaires. C'est ici que naquit notre amitié. Isabel avait alors vingt et un ans. Bien que charmante à la fois par sa personne et par ses manières, (entre nous) elle ne posséda jamais un centième de ma beauté ou de mes prédispositions. Mais Isabel avait vu le monde. Elle avait passé deux ans dans l'un des premiers internats de Londres ; quinze jours à Bath, et avait soupé un soir à Southampton.

« Prenez garde, ma Laura, disait-elle souvent, méfiez-vous des insipides vanités et des distractions oisives de la métropole d'Angleterre ; méfiez-vous des luxes superficiels de Bath et du poisson malodorant de Southampton. »

« Hélas ! m'exclamai-je, comment éviter ces maux auxquels on ne m'exposera jamais ? Quelle chance ai-je de goûter un jour aux distractions de Londres, aux luxes de Bath, ou au poisson malodorant de Southampton ? Moi, qui suis condamnée à gâcher les jours de ma jeunesse et de ma beauté dans un modeste cottage de la vallée de l'Usk. »

Ah ! J'étais alors loin de me douter que bientôt, le destin me forcerait à quitter cemodeste cottage pour les plaisirs trompeurs du monde.

Adieu,
Laura.

Lettre V

Laura à Marianne

Un soir de décembre, alors que mon père, ma mère et moi conversions au coin du feu, nous fûmes soudain stupéfaits d'entendre qu'on frappait brutalement à la porte du cottage.

Mon père sursauta. « Qu'est-ce donc ? demanda-t-il. — Il semblerait que l'on tape à la porte, répondit ma mère. — On dirait bien, en effet, ajoutai-je. — Je suis du même avis, renchérit mon père, quelle violence peu commune à l'égard de notre innocente porte ! — Oui, m'exclamai-je, je ne puis m'empêcher de songer qu'il s'agit de quelqu'un demandant à entrer. — Ceci est un autre débat, répondit-il, nous ne devons prétendre à déterminer les motifs qui poussent une personne à frapper à la porte – même si c'est effectivement le cas, j'en suis en partie convaincu. »

Ici, un coup immense vint interrompre mon père, nous alarmant, ma mère et moi, par la même occasion.

« Ne ferions-nous pas mieux d'aller voir qui va là ? Les domestiques sont sortis, dit-elle. — Je crois que si, répondis-je. — Certainement, ajouta mon père. — Devrions-nous répondre à cet instant ? proposa ma mère. — Le plus tôt sera le mieux, déclara-t-il. — Oh ! Ne perdons pas de temps », m'écriai-je.

Un troisième coup plus violent que jamais résonna durement à nos oreilles.

« Je suis certaine que l'on frappe à la porte, déclara ma mère. — Je suis du même avis, répondit mon père. — Il me semble que les domestiques sont de retour, je crois entendre Mary se diriger vers la porte, dis-je. — Parfait, s'écria mon père, je suis impatient de connaître l'identité de notre visiteur. »

J'avais raison dans mes conjectures, puisque Mary entra à cet instant dans la pièce, nous informant qu'à la porte attendaient un jeune homme et son domestique, qui avaient perdu leur chemin, souffraient du froid, et nous priaient de bien vouloir les laisser se réchauffer auprès du feu.

« N'allez-vous pas les laisser entrer ? dis-je. — Vous n'y voyez pas d'objection, ma chère ? demanda mon père. — Pas le moins du monde, répondit ma mère. »

Mary, sans attendre davantage d'instructions, nous quitta immédiatement pour revenir en compagnie du plus bel et aimable jeune homme qui eût paru devant mes yeux. Quant au domestique, elle le garda pour elle.

D'une grande sensibilité naturelle, j'avais déjà été grandement affectée par les souffrances du malheureux étranger, et il me suffit de le contempler pour comprendre que de lui dépendraient désormais les joies et tristesses de ma vie future.

Adieu,
Laura.

Lettre VI

Laura à Marianne

Le noble jeune homme nous informa que son nom était Lindsay – cependant, j'ai mes raisons pour le garder secret et recourir plutôt à celui de Talbot. Il nous annonça qu'il était le fils d'un baronnet anglais, que sa mère s'était éteinte bien des années plus tôt et qu'il avait une sœur de taille moyenne.

« Mon père, continua-t-il, est un vil et misérable mercenaire – ce n'est qu'en compagnie d'amis si chers ici rassemblés que je trahirais ainsi ses échecs. Vos vertus, aimable Polydore (s'adressant à mon père), les vôtres, chère Claudia, et les vôtres, charmante Laura, inspirent ma confiance. »

Nous acquiesçâmes.

« Mon père, séduit par le faux éclat de la fortune et par l'apparat trompeur du titre, insista pour donner ma main à Lady Dorothea. Non jamais, m'exclamai-je. Lady Dorothea est charmante et agréable ; je ne lui préfère aucune autre femme ; mais sachez, monsieur, que je refuse de l'épouser pour satisfaire vos désirs. Non ! Jamais il ne sera dit que j'ai obéi à mon père. »

Nous admirâmes tous la noble virilité de sa réponse. Il poursuivit.

« Sir Edward s'en étonna ; peut-être n'avait-il pas imaginé rencontrer une opposition aussi vive à sa volonté. "Edward, dit-il, d'où, pour l'amour de Dieu, sortez-vous donc un tel charabia ? Je vous soupçonne d'avoir étudié des romans." Je rechignai à répondre ; cela n'aurait pas été digne de moi. J'enfourchai mon cheval, et suivi de mon fidèle William, je décidai de me rendre chez mes tantes.

« La demeure de mon père se trouve dans le comté du Bedfordshire, celle de mes tantes dans le Middlesex, et bien que je me flatte de maîtriser de manière acceptable la géographie, je ne sais point comment, mais je me retrouvai aux portes de cette magnifique vallée que j'apprends être située dans le sud du pays de Galles, alors que je pensais arriver chez mes parentes.

« Après avoir vagabondé quelque temps sur les berges de l'Usk sans trouver mon chemin, je commençai à me lamenter de mon cruel destin de la manière la plus amère et la plus pathétique qui soit. Il faisait désormais tout à fait nuit, pas une étoile ne brillait pour guider mes pas, et je ne sais ce qu'il serait advenu de moi si je n'avais point discerné au loin, dans les ténèbres, une lumière, qui, lorsque je m'approchai, se révéla être l'éclat joyeux de votre feu de cheminée. Devant les malheurs qui s'abattaient sur moi – à savoir la peur, le froid et la faim –, je n'hésitai point à quérir l'hospitalité qu'on finit par m'accorder ; et à présent, mon adorable Laura, continua-t-il en prenant ma main, quand pourrai-je espérer recevoir la récompense de toutes les douloureuses souffrances qui m'ont accablé par amour pour vous, l'objet de ma tendresse depuis toujours. Oh ! Quand me récompenserez-vous de votre personne ?

— Dès à présent, cher et aimable Edward, répondis-je. » Nous fûmes immédiatement unis par mon père, qui, même s'il n'avait jamais pris les ordres, avait été instruit par l'Église.

Adieu,
Laura.

Lettre VII

Laura à Marianne

Nous ne restâmes que quelques jours dans la vallée de l'Usk. Après des adieux émouvants à mon père, ma mère, et mon Isabel, j'accompagnai Edward chez ses tantes dans le Middlesex. Philippa nous reçut avec toutes les expressions d'un amour affectueux. Mon arrivée était en effet pour elle une surprise des plus agréables, car non seulement elle avait été tenue dans l'ignorance complète du mariage de son neveu, mais elle était également loin de soupçonner l'existence d'une personne si accomplie.

Augusta, la sœur d'Edward, leur rendait visite lorsque nous arrivâmes. Je la trouvai exactement conforme aux descriptions de son frère – elle était de taille moyenne. Si elle me reçut avec la même stupéfaction ; sa cordialité, en revanche, n'égala pas celle de Philippa. Il y avait dans son accueil une froideur désagréable et une réserve austère qui me parurent aussi alarmantes qu'inattendues. Nulle trace, dans ses manières, de cette sensibilité intéressante ni de cette aimable sympathie qui auraient dû distinguer nos présentations lorsqu'elle s'adressa à moi. Son vocabulaire n'était ni chaleureux, ni affectueux, ses salutations ni animées, ni chaleureuses, ses bras n'étaient pas ouverts pour m'accueillir dans son cœur, alors que je m'apprêtais à la serrer contre le mien.

Une brève conversation entre Augusta et son frère, que je surpris par mégarde, renforça mon animosité à son égard, et me convainquit que son cœur n'était pas plus prédisposé aux doux liens de l'amour qu'aux tendres relations de l'amitié.

« Mais croyez-vous que Père soit un jour disposé à accepter une union aussi imprudente ?

— Augusta, répondit le noble jeune homme, je pensais votre opinion de moi meilleure que de me croire capable de me dégrader au point de considérer que l'accord de mon père

– quand il s'agit de mes affaires – puisse avoir une conséquence sur moi, ou même m'intéresser. Dites-moi, Augusta, parlez avec sincérité ; m'avez-vous déjà vu consulter ses désirs, ou suivre ses conseils concernant la moindre bagatelle depuis l'âge de quinze ans ?

— Edward, répondit-elle, vous êtes bien trop timide dans vos louanges. Depuis vos quinze ans ! Mon cher frère, depuis l'âge de cinq ans, je vous acquitte entièrement d'avoir déjà contribué à la satisfaction de votre père. Il demeure que je ne suis point sans appréhender que vous ne soyez bientôt contraint de vous dégrader à vos propres yeux, en devant faire appel pour les besoins de votre femme à la générosité de Sir Edward.

— Jamais, jamais, Augusta, je ne me rabaisserai ainsi. Des besoins ! Quels besoins Laura pourrait-elle bien avoir auxquels il saurait répondre ?

— Seulement les plus insignifiants, ceux des victuailles et de la boisson.

— Les victuailles et la boisson ! répondit mon époux avec un mépris des plus nobles. Et oseriez-vous ainsi croire qu'il n'existe d'autres besoins pour un esprit exalté – comme celui de ma Laura – que les ingrats et indélicats usages que sont boire et manger ?

— À ma connaissance, aucun qui ne soit plus indispensable, répliqua Augusta.

— N'avez-vous donc jamais ressenti la morsure délicieuse de l'amour, Augusta ? Semble-t-il impossible à votre vil et corrompu palais de subsister grâce aux sentiments ? Ne pouvez-vous concevoir le luxe de savourer tous les tourments que peut infliger la pauvreté, en compagnie de l'objet de votre affection la plus tendre ?

— Vous êtes trop ridicule pour être raisonné, déclara Augusta, cependant, peut-être qu'à force vous serez convaincu de… »

C'est ici que je fus empêchée d'entendre la suite de son sermon, par l'arrivée d'une très séduisante jeune femme, qui fut introduite dans la pièce à la porte de laquelle j'écoutais. En l'entendant annoncée par le nom de « Lady Dorothea », je quittai immédiatement mon poste pour la suivre dans le petit salon, car je me souvenais fort bien qu'elle était la demoiselle proposée comme épouse à mon Edward par le cruel et implacable baronnet.

Bien qu'officiellement, Lady Dorothea rendît visite à Philippa et Augusta, j'avais des raisons d'imaginer que son principal dessein – ayant appris la nouvelle du mariage et de l'arrivée d'Edward – était en réalité de me rencontrer.

Je sentis bientôt qu'en dépit de l'élégance et de l'amabilité de sa personne, et de ses manières naturelles et courtoises, elle appartenait, au même titre qu'Augusta, à l'ordre des êtres inférieurs au regard de la délicatesse des émotions, de la tendresse des sentiments, et du raffinement de la sensibilité.

Elle ne resta qu'une demi-heure et à aucun moment au cours de sa visite ne me confia-t-elle de pensées secrètes, ni ne s'enquit des miennes. Ainsi, vous imaginerez fort bien, ma chère Marianne, qu'il me fut impossible de ressentir une affection ardente ou un attachement très sincère à son égard.

Adieu,
Laura.

Lettre VIII

Laura à Marianne, suite

Lady Dorothea venait à peine de nous quitter lorsqu'un visiteur tout aussi inattendu fut annoncé. Il s'agissait de Sir Edward qui, informé par Augusta du mariage de son fils, venait sans doute lui reprocher d'avoir osé s'unir à moi sans qu'il n'en sache rien. Mais Edward, pressentant ses intentions, l'approcha avec un courage héroïque dès qu'il entra dans la pièce, et s'adressa à lui de la manière qui suit :

« Sir Edward, je connais le motif de votre visite ici, vous êtes venu avec le bas dessein de me reprocher l'indissoluble engagement que j'ai pris envers ma Laura sans votre consentement. Mais, monsieur, je me glorifie d'une telle action – c'est en effet ma plus grande fierté que de m'être exposé au déplaisir de mon père ! »

Ainsi déclarant, il saisit ma main, et tandis que Sir Edward, Philippa, et Augusta étaient sans aucun doute possible en train de considérer avec admiration sa vaillante bravoure, il me conduisit du petit salon à la voiture de son père, qui était restée devant la porte, et qui nous éloigna aussitôt de l'emprise de Sir Edward.

Les postillons avaient d'abord reçu l'ordre de prendre la route de Londres. Cependant, aussitôt que nous eûmes réfléchi suffisamment à la question, nous leur demandâmes de nous conduire à M—, le domaine du plus cher ami d'Edward, qui n'était qu'à peu de miles de distance.

Nous atteignîmes M— en quelques heures ; et lorsque nous nous fîmes annoncer, nous fûmes immédiatement reçus par Sophia, l'épouse de l'ami d'Edward. Après avoir été privée pendant trois semaines d'une véritable amie (c'est en ces termes que je réfère à votre mère), imaginez mon transport de joie lorsque je me trouvai devant l'être le plus méritant de ce titre. D'une taille un peu plus haute que la moyenne, Sophia était très élégamment formée. Si une douce langueur parcourait ses adorables traits, elle en augmentait la beauté ; et son esprit était tout entier consacré à la sensibilité et aux émotions. Nous nous jetâmes dans les bras l'une de l'autre et, après avoir échangé des vœux d'amitié réciproque pour le restant de nos vies, nous nous dévoilâmes aussitôt les secrets les plus intimes de nos cœurs – cette délicieuse entreprise fut interrompue par l'entrée d'Augustus, l'ami d'Edward, qui revenait d'une excursion solitaire.

Jamais n'avais-je vu plus émouvante scène que celle des retrouvailles d'Edward et d'Augustus.

« Ma vie ! Mon âme ! s'exclama le premier. — Mon ange adoré ! » répondit le second alors qu'ils s'embrassaient.

C'en fut trop poignant pour les émotions de Sophia et les miennes – nous défaillîmes chacune notre tour sur le sofa.

Adieu,
Laura.

Lettre IX

De la même à la même

Vers la fin du jour, nous reçûmes la missive suivante de la part de Philippa.

« Sir Edward est entré dans une grande fureur après votre abrupt départ ; il a emmené Augusta avec lui dans le Bedfordshire. Bien que je souhaite profiter à nouveau de votre charmante compagnie, je ne songerais à vous arracher à celle d'amis si chers et dignes de mérite. Lorsque votre visite touchera à sa fin, j'espère que vous reviendrez dans les bras de votre Philippa. »

Nous envoyâmes une réponse appropriée à cette note affectueuse et, après l'avoir remerciée pour son aimable invitation, l'assurâmes de notre intention d'y répondre favorablement dès que nous n'aurions nulle part ailleurs où aller. Bien que rien, aux yeux de n'importe quel être raisonnable, n'eût pu sembler plus satisfaisant qu'une réponse si reconnaissante à son invitation, je ne sais ce qu'il se produisit mais elle se montra suffisamment capricieuse pour que notre comportement la contrarie, et quelques semaines plus tard, soit par esprit de revanche devant notre conduite, soit pour échapper à la solitude, elle épousa un jeune coureur de dot illettré. Cette démarche imprudente (bien que nous comprissions qu'elle nous priverait probablement de la fortune que Philippa nous avait laissé espérer en héritage) n'aurait su arracher le moindre soupir à nos esprits exaltés. Pourtant, craignant d'y voir là une source de malheur infini pour la future mariée pleine d'illusions, nous fûmes grandement affectés par l'annonce de l'événement. Les instances affectueuses d'Augustus et de Sophia de considérer leur maison comme la nôtre nous convainquirent facilement de décider de ne plus jamais les quitter. En compagnie d'Edward et de cet aimable couple, je vécus les moments les plus heureux de ma vie ; nous passions le temps de la manière la plus délicieuse qui soit, en déclarations mutuelles d'amitié, et en vœux d'amours inaltérables, sans craindre d'être interrompus par la visite d'intrus désagréables. En effet, Augustus et Sophia avaient, dès leur arrivée dans le voisinage, pris soin d'informer les familles y résidant que, leur bonheur étant centré sur eux-mêmes, ils ne désiraient pas d'autre société. Mais, hélas !, ma chère Marianne, une félicité telle que celle que nous éprouvions était trop parfaite pour durer. Un revers des plus sévères et inattendus anéantit en un instant toute sensation de plaisir. Convaincue comme vous devez l'être après ce que je vous ai déjà écrit au sujet d'Augustus et de Sophia qu'il n'existait pas de couple plus heureux, nul besoin, j'imagine, de vous informer que leur union avait été contraire aux souhaits de cruels et vénaux parents, lesquels avaient vainement tenté, avec une persévérance obstinée, de les forcer à épouser ceux qu'ils avaient toujours haïs. Mais avec une fermeté d'âme héroïque digne d'être contée et admirée, ils avaient tous deux constamment refusé de se soumettre à un tel pouvoir despotique.

Après s'être si noblement désengagés des entraves de l'autorité parentale par un mariage clandestin, ils étaient déterminés à ne jamais faillir à la bonne opinion que le monde avait à présent d'eux en acceptant une proposition de réconciliation que pourraient faire leurs parents – cependant, ils ne furent jamais exposés à cette ultime mise à l'épreuve de leur noble indépendance.

Ils n'étaient mariés que depuis quelques mois quand nous arrivâmes en visite, et n'avaient manqué de rien grâce à une remarquable somme d'argent qu'Augustus avait délicatement subtilisée dans le secrétaire de son père indigne, quelques jours avant son union avec Sophia.

À notre arrivée, leurs dépenses augmentèrent considérablement tandis que les moyens d'y subvenir étaient presque entièrement épuisés. Mais eux – créatures exaltées ! – rechignaient à prendre un moment pour réfléchir à leur détresse pécuniaire, et auraient rougi à l'idée de régler leurs dettes. Hélas ! Quelle ne fut pas leur récompense pour un comportement si désintéressé ! Le bel Augustus fut arrêté et nous fûmes tous ruinés. Une telle trahison, perfide et sans merci, choquera votre douce nature, très chère Marianne, autant qu'elle a alors affecté la délicate sensibilité d'Edward, de Sophia, de votre Laura, ainsi que d'Augustus lui-même. Pour compléter cette barbarie sans commune mesure, nous fûmes informés que la maison allait être saisie. Ah ! Qu'aurions-nous pu faire d'autre que ce que nous fîmes ? Dans un soupir, nous défaillîmes sur le sofa.

Adieu,
Laura.

Lettre X

Laura, suite

Quand nous nous remîmes des effusions accablantes de notre chagrin, Edward souhaita que nous réfléchissions à la conduite la plus prudente à adopter dans notre triste situation tandis qu'il se rendait auprès de son ami emprisonné pour se plaindre de ses malheurs. Nous lui promîmes de le faire, et il se mit en route vers la ville. Durant son absence, nous respectâmes fidèlement son désir, et après une délibération des plus matures, nous conclûmes que la meilleure chose à faire était de quitter la maison, dont les officiers de justice menaçaient à tout moment de prendre possession. Nous attendîmes alors le retour d'Edward avec la plus grande impatience afin de lui faire part du résultat de notre réflexion. Mais nulle trace d'Edward à l'horizon. En vain, nous comptâmes les pénibles secondes de son absence ; en vain nous pleurâmes ; en vain nous soupirâmes ; mais il ne revint pas. Ce fut un coup trop cruel, trop inattendu, pour nos âmes sensibles – nous ne pûmes l'endurer, et il ne nous resta plus qu'à défaillir de nouveau. Enfin, parvenant à rassembler toute la résolution dont j'étais capable, je me levai et, après avoir empaqueté quelques effets pour Sophia et moi-même, je la traînai jusqu'à la voiture que j'avais fait venir et nous prîmes la direction de Londres. Le lieu de résidence d'Augustus se trouvant à moins de douze miles de la ville, nous y arrivâmes bientôt, et à peine étions-nous entrées dans Holboun qu'abaissant une des vitres, je demandai à chaque personne à l'allure décente que nous croisions si elle avait vu mon Edward.

Mais comme nous roulions trop rapidement pour leur laisser le temps de répondre à mes interrogations, je n'obtins que peu, ou plutôt aucune information le concernant.

« Où dois-je vous conduire ? demanda le postillon. — À Newgate, doux jeune homme, pour y voir Augustus, répondis-je. — Oh ! Non, non, s'exclama Sophia, il m'est impossible de me rendre à Newgate ; jamais je ne supporterai la vue de mon Augustus dans un si cruel confinement. Mes sentiments sont suffisamment éprouvés par le récit de sa détresse, je ne supporterais pas de la contempler. »

Comme je m'accordais parfaitement sur la justesse de ses sentiments, l'ordre fut immédiatement donné au postillon de quitter la ville. Vous pourriez sembler surprise, très chère Marianne, que dans la détresse qui m'accablait, privée de tout soutien, et démunie même d'une habitation, pas une seule fois ne me revint en mémoire le souvenir de mon père, de ma mère, ni du cottage paternel dans la vallée de l'Usk. Pour justifier cet apparent oubli, il me faut vous informer d'un détail les concernant dont je n'ai jusqu'à présent pas fait mention. Il s'agit de la mort de mes parents, qui survint quelques semaines après mon départ. Leur décès fit de moi l'héritière légitime de leur maison et de leur fortune. Mais, hélas !, la maison n'avait jamais été leur, et la fortune se limitait à une rente viagère. Voyez ainsi la décadence du monde ! Auprès de votre mère, je serais retournée avec grand plaisir, j'aurais été heureuse de lui présenter ma charmante Sophia, et c'est avec joie que j'aurais passé le restant de mes jours en leur compagnie dans la vallée de l'Usk, si un obstacle à l'exécution d'un rêve si délicieux, n'était pas intervenu ; celui du mariage et du départ de votre mère vers une région reculée d'Irlande.

Adieu,
Laura.

Lettre XI

Laura, suite

« J'ai un parent en Écosse dont je suis certaine qu'il n'hésitera pas à me recevoir », me dit Sophia alors que nous quittions Londres.

« Faut-il que je commande au garçon de nous y conduire ? dis-je – mais aussitôt une pensée me vint et je m'exclamai : Hélas, je crains que le voyage ne soit trop long pour les chevaux. »

Cependant, peu au fait en matière de performances équestres, je consultai le postillon qui fut entièrement de mon avis. Ainsi, nous décidâmes de changer de chevaux en arrivant à la prochaine ville, et de répéter cette manœuvre pour le reste du voyage. Lorsque nous parvinrent à la dernière auberge de notre parcours, qui ne se trouvait qu'à quelques miles de la demeure du parent de Sophia, par peur de lui imposer la surprise de notre société spontanée, nous rédigeâmes une note très élégante et très bien tournée contenant le récit de notre situation démunie et tragique, ainsi que notre intention de passer quelques mois auprès de lui en Écosse. À peine avions-nous envoyé notre missive que nous nous apprêtâmes à la suivre en personne, et c'est à cet effet que nous nous remettions en route lorsque notre attention fut distraite par l'arrivée dans la cour de l'auberge d'une voiture couronnée suivie de quatre autres. Un gentleman d'un âge considérablement avancé en sortit. À son apparition, je me trouvai grandement affectée, et à peine l'avais-je regardé une seconde fois qu'une sympathie instinctive chuchota à mon cœur que j'avais devant moi mon grand-père. Convaincue qu'aucune erreur n'était possible dans ma conjecture, d'un bond je m'échappai de la voiture à bord de laquelle je venais de monter, me jetai à genoux devant lui, et le suppliai de me reconnaître comme sa petite-fille. Il sursauta, et après avoir attentivement examiné mes traits, m'invita à me lever et, m'enlaçant de ses bras de grand-père, il s'exclama :

« Vous reconnaître ! Oui, cher portrait de ma Laurina et de la fille de Laurina, douce image de ma Claudia et de la mère de ma Claudia, je vous reconnais comme la fille de la première, et la petite-fille de la seconde. »

Alors qu'il m'embrassait tendrement, Sophia, restée interdite par mon départ précipité, entra dans la pièce à ma recherche. À peine eut-elle attiré le regard du vénérable pair qu'il s'écria avec toutes les expressions de la surprise :

« Voici encore une petite-fille ! Oui, oui, je vois que vous êtes la fille de l'aînée de ma Laurina ; votre ressemblance avec la belle Matilda est une preuve suffisante.

— Oh ! répondit Sophia, quand je vous ai contemplé pour la première fois, l'instinct de la Nature m'a immédiatement soufflé que nous étions parents – mais grand-père ou grand-mère, je n'aurais su le dire. »

Il la prit dans ses bras tendrement, et la porte s'ouvrit sur un jeune homme des plus séduisants. Lord St. Clair sursauta, s'écarta de quelques pas et, les mains en l'air, rugit :

« Un autre petit-enfant ! Quelle heureuse surprise ! Découvrir en l'espace de trois minutes autant de descendants ! Voici, j'en suis certain, Philander, le fils de la troisième fille de ma Laurina, l'aimable Bertha ; il ne manque plus que la présence de Gustavus pour compléter la réunion des petits-enfants de ma Laurina.

— Et le voici, dit un gracieux jeune homme entrant à son tour dans la pièce, voici le Gustavus que vous souhaitiez voir. Je suis le fils d'Agatha, la quatrième et dernière fille de votre Laurina.

— En effet, c'est bien vous, répondit Lord St. Clair. Mais dites-moi, continua-t-il en lançant un regard effrayé vers la porte, ai-je encore d'autres petits-enfants sous ce toit ?
— Aucun, monsieur. — Dans ce cas, je vais sans plus tarder subvenir à vos besoins : voilà quatre billets de cinquante livres, prenez-les et souvenez-vous qu'ainsi faisant, j'ai rempli mon devoir de grand-père. »

Immédiatement, il quitta la pièce, puis l'auberge.

Adieu,
Laura.

Lettre XII

Laura, suite

Il vous sera aisé d'imaginer notre immense surprise devant le départ soudain de Lord St. Clair. « Quel ignoble aïeul ! » s'exclama Sophia. « Un grand-père indigne ! » complétai-je, et immédiatement nous défaillîmes dans les bras l'une de l'autre. Je ne saurais estimer la durée de notre état, mais lorsque nous nous réveillâmes, nous étions seules, et Gustavus, Philander et les billets avaient tous disparu. Alors que nous nous lamentions sur notre cruel destin, la porte s'ouvrit et on annonça Macdonald, le cousin de Sophia.

L'empressement avec lequel il avait accouru à notre secours après avoir reçu notre missive parla si grandement en sa faveur que je n'hésitai pas, dès le premier regard, à déclarer qu'il avait tout d'un ami tendre et compatissant. Hélas ! Il ne méritait point ce nom – car bien qu'à ses dires alarmé par nos malheureuses aventures, il sembla que leur lecture ne lui avait pas arraché un seul soupir, ni ne l'avait poussé à maudire nos étoiles vindicatives. Il dit à Sophia que sa fille insistait pour qu'elle le suive à Macdonald Hall, et qu'en tant qu'amie de sa cousine, il serait également heureux de me voir faire de même. Vers Macdonald Hall, nous partîmes donc, et nous y fûmes reçues avec une grande gentillesse par Janetta, la fille de Macdonald, et maîtresse des lieux. Janetta n'avait que quinze ans ; naturellement bien disposée, dotée d'un cœur sensible et compatissant, elle aurait pu – si ces aimables qualités avaient été encouragées – faire gloire à la nature humaine ; mais, malheureusement, son père ne possédait pas une âme assez exaltée pour admirer une aptitude si prometteuse, et avait par tous les moyens possibles empêché qu'elle ne se développe avec les années. En vérité, il avait même tant effacé la noble sensibilité naturelle de son cœur que son influence l'avait poussée à accepter d'épouser un jeune homme qu'il lui avait recommandé. Le mariage était prévu pour dans quelques mois, et Graham était présent au manoir lorsque nous arrivâmes. Nous devinâmes bien vite son véritable caractère – tant il correspondait à l'image qu'on pouvait se faire d'un prétendant choisi par Macdonald. On disait de lui qu'il était raisonnable, averti et plaisant ; nous ne prétendions pas le juger sur de tels détails, mais comme nous étions convaincues qu'il n'avait pas d'âme, qu'il n'avait jamais lu *Les Souffrances du jeune Werther*, et que sa chevelure ne comportait pas la moindre nuance d'auburn, nous étions certaines que Janetta ne pouvait éprouver nulle affection à son égard, ou tout du moins qu'elle ne le devrait pas. Le fait qu'il ait été choisi par son père jouait tant en sa défaveur que quand bien même il eût mérité son affection, cette seule condition aurait dû aux yeux de Janetta être une raison suffisante pour le refuser. Nous étions déterminées à lui exposer ces circonstances comme de juste et ne doutions pas de rencontrer le succès escompté devant une créature si naturellement bien disposée ; dont les erreurs dans cette affaire n'étaient que le résultat d'un manque de confiance en sa propre opinion et de mépris envers celle de son père. Et en réalité nous trouvâmes chez elle tout ce que nos souhaits les plus sincères auraient pu espérer ; nous n'eûmes nulle difficulté à la convaincre qu'il était impossible qu'elle aimât Graham, et qu'il était de son devoir de désobéir à son père. La seule chose qui la fit hésiter fut notre assertion qu'elle ne pouvait qu'être attachée à un autre. Pendant quelque temps, elle persista à déclarer qu'elle ne connaissait pas d'autre jeune homme pour lequel elle éprouvât la moindre affection ; mais quand nous lui expliquâmes l'impossibilité d'une telle chose, elle concéda qu'en effet, il lui semblait nourrir une préférence pour le capitaine M'Kenrie. Cette confession nous laissa satisfaites, et après avoir énuméré les qualités de M'Kenrie et l'avoir assurée qu'elle était furieusement éprise, nous désirâmes savoir s'il avait jamais déclaré son inclination pour elle.

« Bien loin de l'avoir déclarée, je n'ai pas de raison d'imaginer qu'il en ait jamais ressenti à mon égard, dit Janetta.

— Nul doute, répondit Sophia, qu'il vous adore. Un attachement ne peut être que réciproque. Ne vous a-t-il jamais contemplée avec admiration, n'a-t-il pas posé sa main sur la vôtre, laissé s'échapper une larme, puis quitté la pièce abruptement ?

— Jamais, pour autant que je me souvienne. S'il a en effet toujours quitté la pièce lorsque sa visite touchait à sa fin, ce ne fut pas d'une manière particulièrement abrupte, ni sans me saluer.

— C'est que, ma chère, dis-je, vous avez fait erreur, car il est absolument impossible qu'il ne vous ait pas laissée avec confusion, désespoir et précipitation. Songez-y un instant, Janetta, et vous verrez à quel point l'idée est absurde qu'il ait pu vous saluer, ou se comporter comme n'importe qui d'autre à votre égard. »

Après avoir réglé ce détail à notre entière satisfaction, il ne nous restait qu'à déterminer la façon d'informer M'Kenrie de l'opinion favorable qu'entretenait Janetta à son endroit... Nous tombâmes enfin d'accord sur l'envoi d'une lettre anonyme que Sophia rédigea de la manière suivante.

« Ô heureux amant de la belle Janetta, ô aimable maître du cœur dont la main est destinée à un autre, pourquoi reporter la confession de votre attachement ? Oh ! Songez que quelques semaines mettront fin au moindre espoir flatteur que vous entretenez, en unissant la malheureuse victime de la cruauté de son père à l'exécrable et détesté Graham.

Hélas ! Pourquoi participer si cruellement à son malheur futur ainsi qu'au vôtre en retardant l'expression du projet qui occupe sans nul doute depuis bien longtemps votre imagination ? Une union secrète assurerait si vite votre bonheur commun. »

L'aimable M'Kenrie, dont la pudeur – comme il nous l'assura plus tard – l'avait seule poussé à dissimuler si longtemps l'ardeur de ses sentiments pour Janetta, en recevant ce billet, fut porté par les ailes de l'amour jusqu'à Macdonald Hall, et plaida avec tant de force l'attachement qu'elle lui inspirait, qu'après plusieurs entretiens, Sophia et moi eûmes la satisfaction de les voir s'en aller pour Gretna-Green[1], ville qu'ils avaient choisie pour célébrer leurs noces, la préférant curieusement à n'importe quelle autre en dépit de la distance considérable qui la séparait de Macdonald Hall.

Adieu,
Laura.

Lettre XIII

Laura, suite

Plusieurs heures s'étaient écoulées avant que Macdonald et Graham ne commencent à entretenir des soupçons quant à leur disparition. Et ils ne l'auraient peut-être même pas suspectée sans ce léger incident. En réussissant par hasard à ouvrir un tiroir de la bibliothèque de Macdonald avec une de ses propres clefs, Sophia découvrit qu'il y conservait des papiers d'importance, et parmi eux des billets de banque d'un montant considérable. Elle partagea cette découverte avec moi ; et, nous accordant à dire qu'il ne serait que justice de priver un misérable tel que Macdonald d'un argent probablement obtenu par des moyens malhonnêtes, il fut décidé que lorsque l'une de nous se trouverait par hasard à cet endroit, nous n'hésiterions pas à sortir un billet de banque ou plus du tiroir.

---

[1]. Village du Sud de l'Écosse célèbre pour la possibilité qu'il offrait aux mineurs de se marier sans l'autorisation de leurs parents. (NdT)

Ce projet plein de bonnes intentions fut mis à exécution à de nombreuses reprises ; mais – hélas ! – le jour même où Janetta s'échappa, alors que Sophia s'emparait majestueusement du cinquième billet de banque pour le ranger dans sa propre bourse, elle fut soudain impertinemment interrompue par l'entrée de Macdonald lui-même, de la manière la plus abrupte et précipitée. Sophia, qui pensait naturellement que sa douceur charmeuse pouvait, si l'occasion l'exigeait, en appeler à la dignité de son sexe, adopta immédiatement un air interdit, et décochant un regard indigné à l'intention du fautif téméraire, demanda d'une voix hautaine quelle raison valait que sa retraite fût si insolemment interrompue. Macdonald, qui n'afficha pas la moindre rougeur, et sans même tenter de s'innocenter du crime dont on l'accusait, entreprit vilement de reprocher à Sophia de l'avoir ignoblement détroussé de son argent...

L'honneur de Sophia en fut blessé – « Misérable !, s'écria-t-elle en replaçant vivement le billet de banque dans le tiroir, comment osez-vous m'accuser d'un tel acte, dont la seule pensée me fait rougir ? » L'infâme mesquin, demeurant incrédule, continuait de réprimander Sophia, offensée comme de juste par un langage si chargé d'opprobre qu'il finit par provoquer grandement la douce bonté de sa nature au point de la forcer à se venger en lui révélant la fugue romantique de Janetta, ainsi que le rôle prévalant que nous avions tenu dans l'affaire.

C'est à ce moment de leur querelle que je pénétrai dans la bibliothèque et je fus, comme vous l'imaginerez fort bien, tout aussi offensée que Sophia devant les accusations insensées du méprisable et malveillant Macdonald.

« Vil mécréant ! m'écriai-je. Comment pouvez-vous avoir l'audace de souiller la réputation immaculée d'une si splendide excellence ? Au point où vous en êtes, pourquoi ne pas en plus mettre en doute mon innocence ?

— Soyez rassurée, madame, répondit-il, je la suspecte en effet, et ainsi je me dois d'exiger que vous quittiez toutes deux cette maison dans la demi-heure.

— C'est avec joie que nous partirons, répondit Sophia, nos cœurs vous haïssent depuis longtemps, et seule notre amitié pour votre fille nous aura persuadées de rester si longtemps sous votre toit.

— Quelle grande preuve d'amitié envers ma fille que de la jeter dans les bras d'un coureur de dot sans foi ni loi !

— Oui, m'exclamai-je, en dépit de tous nos malheurs, nous aurons au moins la consolation de songer que par ce seul acte d'amitié envers Janetta, nous sommes amplement déchargées de la moindre obligation que nous aurions due à son père.

— Cela doit être une idée bien gratifiante pour vos esprits exaltés. »

Dès que nous eûmes rassemblé nos toilettes et nos effets, nous quittâmes Macdonald Hall, et après avoir marché environ un mile et demi, nous nous assîmes sur la rive d'une rivière limpide et claire pour rafraîchir nos membres exténués. L'endroit était propice à la méditation. Un bosquet de grands ormes nous protégeait à l'est ; un lit de hautes orties à l'ouest. Devant nous courait le murmure de l'eau et derrière nous la grande route. Nous étions d'humeur contemplative et disposées à apprécier la beauté du lieu. Le silence qui avait un moment régné entre nous fut finalement brisé lorsque je m'exclamai :

« Quel charmant paysage ! Hélas, pourquoi Edward et Augustus ne sont-ils pas là pour admirer sa beauté avec nous ?

— Ah ! Ma Laura adorée, s'écria Sophia, par pitié, abstenez-vous de rappeler à mon souvenir la triste situation de mon mari emprisonné. Hélas, que ne donnerais-je pas pour connaître le destin de mon Augustus ! Pour savoir s'il est toujours à Newgate, ou s'il a déjà été pendu. Mais jamais je ne saurais conquérir assez de force pour me résoudre à m'enquérir de son état. Oh, je vous en conjure, ne me laissez jamais vous entendre répéter son nom adoré. Cela m'affecte tant. Je ne puis supporter de l'entendre mentionné et d'être si profondément blessée.

— Pardonnez-moi, ma Sophia, de vous avoir si innocemment offensée », répondis-je. Puis, changeant de conversation, je la priai d'admirer la noble stature des ormes qui nous abritaient, à l'est, du zéphyr.

« Hélas ! ma Laura, répondit-elle, évitez un tel sujet mélancolique, je vous en prie. Ne blessez pas davantage mon cœur sensible par vos observations de ces ormes. Ils me rappellent mon Augustus. Comme eux, il était haut, majestueux, et il possédait cette noble stature que vous admirez. »

Je demeurai silencieuse, par crainte de causer involontairement une nouvelle détresse en abordant un sujet qui lui rappellerait encore Augustus.

« Pourquoi ne parlez-vous donc plus, ma Laura ? dit-elle après une courte pause. Je ne puis souffrir ce silence, vous ne pouvez m'abandonner à mes propres réflexions ; elles ne cessent de rejoindre Augustus.

— Quel ciel magnifique ! Comme l'azur est charmant, ainsi délicatement strié de blanc !

— Oh ! Ma Laura, répondit-elle en détournant vivement le regard qu'elle avait lancé vers le ciel. N'amplifiez point ma détresse en attirant mon attention sur un objet qui me rappelle si cruellement le gilet de satin bleu rayé de blanc de mon Augustus ! Par pitié pour votre malheureuse amie, évitez un sujet si pénible. »

Que faire alors ? Les sentiments qu'éprouvait Sophia à ce moment étaient si exquis, et la tendresse qu'elle ressentait pour Augustus si poignante que je n'eus pas la force d'orienter la conversation vers un autre sujet, craignant avec justesse de réveiller d'une manière imprévue sa douleur pour le sort de son mari. Et pourtant, le silence aurait été cruel ; elle m'avait enjoint à parler.

De ce dilemme je fus heureusement délivrée par un incident fort à propos ; par chance, sur la route qui courait derrière nous, la voiture d'un gentleman se renversa. Ce fut un accident des plus heureux car il détourna l'attention de Sophia des réflexions mélancoliques dans lesquelles elle était plongée. Nous quittâmes immédiatement nos places et accourûmes au secours de ceux qui, quelques instants plus tôt, étaient élevés si haut à bord d'un phaéton à la dernière mode, mais se trouvaient maintenant aussi bas que terre, affalés dans la poussière.

« Quels riches sujets propices aux réflexions sur le caractère instable des plaisirs de ce bas monde que ceux du phaéton et de la vie du cardinal Wolsey ! » dis-je à Sophia alors que nous nous empressions vers le lieu de l'accident.

Elle n'eut pas le temps de me répondre car chaque pensée était désormais accaparée par le terrible spectacle qui s'étendait sous nos yeux. Nous fûmes frappées à la vue de deux gentlemen élégamment vêtus qui baignaient dans leur sang, et quand nous approchâmes, nous reconnûmes Edward et Augustus. Oui, très chère Marianne, nos maris. Sophia poussa un cri avant de s'évanouir au sol ; je hurlai et perdis immédiatement la tête. Nous demeurâmes ainsi privées de nos esprits, et en les regagnant les perdîmes à nouveau. Une heure et un quart durant, nous fûmes victimes de cette malheureuse situation – Sophia défaillait à chaque instant et une folie passagère s'emparait de moi tout aussi souvent. Enfin, un grognement du malheureux Edward (qui seul conservait une parcelle de vie) nous ramena à nous-mêmes. En les imaginant encore en vie, nous aurions été plus parcimonieuses dans notre deuil, mais comme nous avions supposé qu'ils n'étaient plus, nous savions qu'il ne restait plus rien à faire que ce que nous faisions. À peine avions-nous entendu le grognement de mon Edward que, reportant nos lamentations, nous accourûmes auprès du cher jeune homme et, nous agenouillant chacune à son côté, l'implorâmes de ne point mourir.

« Laura, dit-il en posant sur moi son regard désormais alangui, je crains d'avoir été renversé. »

Je fus emplie de joie de le trouver si raisonnable.

« Oh ! Parlez-moi, Edward. Je vous en conjure ! Avant de mourir, dites-moi ce qu'il vous est arrivé depuis le triste jour où Augustus a été arrêté et où nous avons été séparés.

— Je le promets », dit-il – et voulant pousser un profond soupir, il rendit son dernier.

Sophia défaillit à l'instant. Mon propre deuil fut plus audible, ma voix trembla, mes yeux adoptèrent un regard vide, mon visage se fit plus blanc que la mort, et mon esprit en fut considérablement perturbé.

« Ne me parlez plus de phaétons, dis-je, affolée et incohérente dans mon délire. Qu'on m'apporte un violon. Je jouerai pour apaiser ses heures de mélancolie – prenez garde, douces nymphes, aux éclairs de Cupidon et aux flèches perçantes de Jupiter – regardez ce bosquet de sapins – je vois un gigot – on m'a dit qu'Edward n'était pas mort ; mais on m'a dupée – on l'a pris pour un concombre. » Je persistai dans ces exclamations qu'avait causées la mort de mon Edward. Mon délire dura deux heures, et j'aurais poursuivi dans ma folie – n'étant pas le moins du monde fatiguée – si Sophia, recouvrant ses esprits, ne m'avait pas fait remarquer que la nuit approchait et que la rosée commençait à tomber.

« Où aller, demandai-je, pour nous protéger des deux ? — Dans ce cottage blanc », répondit-elle en désignant une maisonnée propre qui s'élevait parmi les ormes et que je n'avais pas vue plus tôt.

J'acquiesçai et nous partîmes dans sa direction. Nous frappâmes à la porte, une vieille femme ouvrit ; quand nous lui demandâmes l'hospitalité pour la nuit, elle nous informa que sa maison était petite, qu'elle ne comportait que deux chambres, cependant, nous étions les bienvenues dans l'une d'elles. Satisfaites, nous suivîmes la généreuse femme à l'intérieur, où nous fûmes grandement réconfortées par la vue d'un feu de cheminée. Elle était veuve et n'avait qu'une fille, qui venait d'avoir dix-sept ans – un des meilleurs âges, mais, hélas !, elle était tout à fait laide et portait le nom de Bridget... Impossible alors de formuler des attentes pour elle – on pouvait supposer qu'elle ne possédât ni idées exaltées, ni sentiments délicats, ni sensibilité raffinée – ; elle n'était rien de plus qu'une demoiselle au bon caractère, polie et serviable ; c'est pourquoi nous ne pouvions pas même la détester – elle ne pouvait être qu'objet de mépris.

Adieu,
Laura.

Lettre XIV

Laura, suite

Armez-vous, ma tendre et jeune amie, de toute la philosophie dont vous êtes maîtresse ; rassemblez toute la force d'âme dont vous êtes capable car – hélas ! – à la lecture des pages qui suivent, votre cœur sensible sera plus que jamais mis à l'épreuve. Ah ! Que sont les malheurs que je connus avant et dont je vous ai déjà fait le récit à côté de celui que je m'apprête à vous conter ! La mort de mon père, de ma mère et de mon mari, bien que presque trop difficile à supporter pour ma nature délicate, n'étaient que détails en comparaison de la mésaventure que je vais vous narrer. Le matin qui suivit notre arrivée au cottage, Sophia se plaignit d'une douleur violente dans ses membres, accompagnée d'une désagréable migraine. Elle pensa qu'il s'agissait des conséquences d'un coup de froid attrapé lors de ses nombreux évanouissements en plein air, la veille, alors que la rosée tombait. Je craignais que ce ne soit que trop probablement vrai ; car comment expliquer que j'échappasse à la même indisposition, sinon en supposant que les exercices corporels dont j'avais été victime pendant mes délires avaient si efficacement réchauffé et fait circuler mon sang qu'ils m'avaient protégée de la moite froideur de la nuit, tandis que Sophia, étendue et absolument immobile sur le sol, avait dû être exposée à leur sévérité. Je fus très sérieusement alarmée par sa maladie, aussi triviale qu'elle puisse vous sembler, car une certaine sensibilité instinctive me soufflait qu'elle lui serait fatale.

Hélas ! Mes craintes n'étaient que trop justifiées ; son état empira et chaque jour je m'inquiétai davantage. Enfin, elle fut contrainte de se confiner au lit que lui avait alloué notre bonne hôtesse. Son trouble se mua en une phtisie galopante qui l'emporta en quelques jours. Dans mes lamentations – dont vous imaginerez la violence –, je trouvai pourtant à me consoler en songeant à toute l'attention que je lui avais consacrée pendant sa maladie. J'avais pleuré chaque jour sur son corps, j'avais lavé son joli visage de mes larmes et je n'avais cessé de presser ses blanches mains dans les miennes.

« Ma Laura adorée, me dit-elle quelques heures avant de mourir, apprenez de mon triste sort et évitez la conduite imprudente qui m'y a menée... méfiez-vous des malaises... même si sur le moment ils semblent rafraîchissants et plaisants, à la fin, croyez-moi, si trop souvent répétés à des saisons inappropriées, ils s'avéreront destructeurs pour votre constitution... Puisse mon destin vous enseigner cela. Je meurs martyre du chagrin causé par la perte d'Augustus... Un évanouissement fatal m'a coûté la vie... Méfiez-vous des évanouissements, chère Laura... un élan de folie n'est pas aussi néfaste d'un quart ; c'est un exercice pour le corps et s'il n'est pas trop violent, j'ose dire qu'il est bon pour la santé – rendez-vous folle aussi souvent qu'il vous plaira, mais ne défaillez point. »

Ce furent là les derniers mots qu'elle m'adressa... Un conseil prodigué sur son lit de mort à sa Laura affligée, qui plus que jamais y adhéra sincèrement.

Après avoir accompagné mon amie jusqu'à sa tombe prématurée en pleurant, je quittai immédiatement – bien qu'il fût tard dans la nuit – le village honni dans lequel elle avait rendu l'âme, et près duquel avaient expiré mon mari et Augustus. Je ne m'étais pas éloignée de beaucoup que je fus dépassée par une diligence à bord de laquelle je pris place, dans l'idée de rejoindre Édimbourg, où j'espérais trouver un ami compatissant pour me recevoir et me consoler de mes afflictions.

Il faisait si noir lorsque je montai dans la voiture que je ne pus distinguer mes compagnons de voyage ; je perçus seulement qu'ils étaient nombreux. Sans me soucier d'apprendre quoi que ce fût à leur sujet, je m'abandonnai à mes propres réflexions tragiques. Un silence régnait, que seuls venaient interrompre les ronflements sonores et réguliers de l'un des voyageurs.

« Quel vil illettré doit être cet homme ! pensai-je. Quel manque absolu de raffinement et de délicatesse de frapper nos sens de la sorte par un bruit si brutal ! Il doit être capable des actions les plus horribles, c'est certain ! Il n'existe pas de crime trop noir pour un tel personnage ! »

Ainsi raisonnai intérieurement – à l'instar, je n'en doute pas, de mes compagnons de voyage.

Enfin, l'aube me permit de contempler le scélérat sans scrupule qui avait si violemment agressé mes oreilles. Il s'agissait de Sir Edward, le père de feu mon mari. À côté de lui était assise Augusta, et sur ma banquette se trouvaient votre mère et Lady Dorothea. Imaginez ma surprise en me voyant ainsi entourée de mes anciennes connaissances ! Aussi grand que fût mon étonnement, il s'amplifia davantage lorsque, en regardant par la fenêtre, je vis à l'avant le mari de Philippa, ainsi que Philippa, et à l'arrière Philander et Gustavus. « Oh ! Seigneur, m'exclamai-je, serait-il possible que je me trouvasse par hasard entourée de mes plus proches parents et connaissances ? » Ces mots éveillèrent le reste des voyageurs, et tous les yeux se tournèrent vers le coin que j'occupais.

« Oh ! Mon Isabel, continuai-je en me jetant dans ses bras par-dessus Lady Dorothea, accueillez une fois encore en votre sein la malheureuse Laura. Hélas ! Quand nous nous quittâmes dans la vallée de l'Usk, j'étais portée par la joie de mon union nouvelle avec le meilleur des Edward ; j'avais alors un père et une mère, et n'avais jamais connu la moindre mésaventure – à présent me voilà privée de tous mes amis sauf vous.

— Comment ! m'interrompit Augusta. Mon frère est-il donc mort ? Parlez, je vous l'ordonne ! Qu'est-il advenu de lui ?

— Oui, nymphe froide et insensible, répondis-je, mon soupirant malchanceux, votre frère, n'est plus, et vous pouvez désormais vous glorifier d'être l'héritière de la fortune de Sir Edward. »

Bien que l'ayant toujours méprisée depuis le jour où j'avais surpris sa conversation avec mon Edward, par courtoisie je me pliai à ses prières ainsi qu'à celles de Sir Edward et les informai de la triste affaire. Ils en furent grandement frappés – même le cœur implacable de Sir Edward et celui insensible d'Augusta furent émus par ce conte malheureux. À la demande de votre mère, je leur racontai toutes les autres mésaventures dont j'avais été victime depuis notre séparation. L'emprisonnement d'Augustus et l'absence d'Edward, notre arrivée en Écosse, la stupéfiante rencontre avec notre grand-père et nos cousins, notre visite à Macdonald Hall, le service précieux que nous y rendîmes à Janetta, l'ingratitude de son père qui en découla... son comportement inhumain, ses accusations infondées, la manière barbare dont il nous traita en nous obligeant à quitter son toit... nos lamentations sur la perte d'Edward et d'Augustus et enfin la terrible mort de ma compagne adorée.

La pitié et la surprise se dessinèrent très nettement sur le visage de votre mère, durant tout mon récit, mais je suis navrée de vous dire, en éternel reproche à sa sensibilité, que la seconde fut infiniment prédominante. Pis, aussi irréprochable qu'eût été ma conduite à travers mes malheurs, elle prétendit trouver mon comportement fautif dans nombre des situations où je m'étais retrouvée. Comme je savais raisonnablement avoir toujours agi d'une manière qui faisait honneur à mes sentiments et à mon raffinement, je ne prêtai qu'une attention minime à ses propos, et demandai qu'elle satisfasse ma curiosité en m'apprenant comment elle était arrivée ici, au lieu de souiller ma réputation immaculée de ses blâmes injustifiés. Dès qu'elle se soumit à mes souhaits et m'eut rendu un récit détaillé de tout ce qu'il lui était advenu depuis notre séparation (détails dont, si vous n'avez pas encore connaissance, votre mère pourra vous faire part), je priai Augusta d'en faire autant pour elle-même, Sir Edward et Lady Dorothea.

Elle me dit qu'ayant toujours eu un goût prononcé pour les beautés de la nature, sa curiosité de contempler les scènes délicieuses déployées dans cette partie du monde avait été tant éveillée par le *Voyage dans les Highlands* de Gilpin qu'elle avait convaincu son père d'entreprendre un tour de l'Écosse et avait persuadé Lady Dorothea de les accompagner. Ils étaient arrivés à Édimbourg quelques jours plus tôt, et de là avaient conduit des excursions quotidiennes dans les paysages avoisinant à bord de la voiture que nous occupions à présent, et revenaient justement de l'une de ces excursions. Mes questions suivantes concernaient Philippa et son mari ; j'appris ainsi que ce dernier, ayant dilapidé toute sa dot, s'adonnait désormais à une activité dans laquelle il avait toujours excellé, la conduite, et après avoir vendu tous leurs biens à l'exception de leur voiture, il louait à présent ses services. Pour éviter de rencontrer ses anciennes connaissances, il s'était rendu à Édimbourg, d'où il assurait un jour sur deux des trajets vers Sterling. Philippa, entretenant toujours de l'affection pour son mari ingrat, l'avait suivi en Écosse et l'accompagnait généralement dans ses allers-retours. « Ce n'est que pour remplir un peu leurs poches, continua Augusta, que mon père a voyagé à bord de leur voiture pour contempler le paysage depuis notre arrivée en Écosse — car il aurait certainement été bien plus plaisant de visiter les Highlands en voiture privée plutôt que d'aller et venir d'Édimbourg à Sterling tous les jours dans une diligence bondée et incommode comme celle-ci. » Je m'accordai parfaitement avec son sentiment sur cette histoire, et blâmai secrètement Sir Edward de sacrifier ainsi le bon plaisir de sa fille pour une vieille femme ridicule dont la folie d'avoir épousé un homme si jeune méritait d'être punie. Son attitude, cependant, était tout à fait en accord avec son caractère général ; car que pouvait-on attendre d'un homme qui ne possédait pas une once de sensibilité, qui connaissait à peine le sens du mot compassion, et qui ronflait ?

Adieu,
Laura.

Lettre XV

Laura, suite

Quand nous arrivâmes dans la ville où nous devions petit-déjeuner, j'étais déterminée à m'entretenir avec Philander et Gustavus, et dans ce dessein, dès que je descendis de voiture, je la contournai pour les rejoindre à l'arrière et m'inquiétai avec tendresse de leur bonne santé, exprimant mes craintes quant à l'inconfort de leur situation. Ils semblèrent dans un premier temps confus par mon apparition, redoutant certainement que je ne leur demande des comptes pour l'argent que notre grand-père m'avait laissé et dont ils m'avaient injustement privée, mais comme je ne mentionnai rien de l'affaire, ils m'invitèrent à prendre place avec eux sur le porte-bagages pour y poursuivre notre conversation plus confortablement. Je les y rejoignis, et pendant que le reste de notre société engloutissait thé vert et tartines beurrées, bien plus raffinés et sentimentaux, nous festoyâmes des confidences de la conversation. Je les informai de tout ce qu'il m'était advenu au cours de ma vie, et à ma demande ils me racontèrent chaque incident des leurs.

« Comme vous le savez déjà, nous sommes les fils des deux plus jeunes filles que Lord St. Clair eut avec Laurina, une danseuse d'opéra italienne. Aucune de nos mères ne put avec certitude nous apprendre l'identité de nos pères, même si la rumeur donne Philander comme le fils d'un maçon du nom de Philip Jones, et moi-même comme celui de Gregory Staves, corsetier à Édimbourg. Cependant, ceci est de peu de conséquence, car nos mères ne furent jamais mariées à aucun des deux, ainsi n'ont-ils jeté aucun déshonneur sur notre sang, qui est des plus anciens et des plus purs. Bertha (la mère de Philander) et Agatha (la mienne) vécurent toujours ensemble ; aucune n'était très riche ; leurs fortunes rassemblées s'élevaient à l'origine à neuf mille livres, mais elles avaient pour habitude de dépenser plus que leur rente, si bien que quand nous eûmes quinze ans, elle était réduite à neuf cents. Ces neuf cents livres, elles les conservaient dans un tiroir de la table qui trônait dans notre salon, car il était plus commode de les garder à portée de main. Peut-être à cause de cette circonstance, de la facilité qu'il y avait à les prendre, ou à cause d'un désir d'indépendance, ou bien d'un excès de sensibilité dont nous étions remarquablement dotés – il m'est impossible de le déterminer –, toujours est-il que lorsque nous atteignîmes l'année de nos quinze ans, nous nous emparâmes des neuf cents livres, puis disparûmes. Ayant gagné cette somme, nous étions déterminés à l'employer avec économie et à ne pas la dépenser avec folie ou extravagance. Ainsi, nous la divisâmes en neuf parts, et allouâmes la première aux victuailles, la deuxième à la boisson, la troisième à la maison, la quatrième aux voitures, la cinquième aux chevaux, la sixième aux domestiques, la septième à notre amusement, la huitième à notre garde-robe, et la neuvième aux boucles de chaussure en argent. Ayant arrangé de la sorte nos dépenses pour deux mois – car nous avions l'intention de faire durer les neuf cents livres aussi longtemps –, nous nous pressâmes en direction de Londres où nous eûmes la bonne fortune de les dépenser en sept semaines et une journée, ce qui était six jours de moins que nos prévisions. Dès que nous nous fûmes si gaiement désencombrés du poids d'une telle somme, nous commençâmes à envisager un retour auprès de nos mères, mais apprenant par hasard qu'elles étaient toutes deux mortes de faim, nous abandonnâmes ce dessein et décidâmes de nous engager dans une compagnie ambulante de comédiens, puisque nous avions toujours eu un penchant pour la scène. Dès lors, nous proposâmes nos services, qui furent acceptés. Notre troupe n'était point grande, en effet, et se composait du directeur, de sa femme et de nous-mêmes, mais nous étions ainsi moins nombreux à partager les gains, et le seul inconvénient était la rareté des pièces que, par manque de comédiens pour incarner tous les rôles, nous pouvions jouer. Cependant, nous ne nous encombrions pas de tels détails. Une de nos performances les plus admirées était celle de *Macbeth*, dans laquelle nous étions exceptionnels. Le directeur y tenait le rôle de Banquo, sa femme Lady Macbeth. Je jouais les trois sorcières et Philander le reste. À dire vrai, cette tragédie n'était pas seulement la meilleure, mais aussi la seule pièce à notre répertoire ; et après des représentations dans toute l'Angleterre et le pays de Galles, nous arrivâmes en Écosse pour la montrer au reste de la Grande-Bretagne. Nous avions pris nos quartiers dans cette même ville où vous vîntes et où nous fîmes la connaissance de votre grand-père ; nous étions dans la cour lorsque sa voiture entra, et reconnaissant par ses armoiries son propriétaire, et sachant que Lord St. Clair était notre grand-père, nous décidâmes d'obtenir quelque chose de lui en lui révélant notre lien. Vous savez vous-même le succès de cette entreprise. Ayant ainsi gagné deux cents livres, nous quittâmes la ville sur-le-champ, laissant le directeur et sa femme interpréter seuls *Macbeth*, et prîmes la route pour Sterling, où nous dépensâmes notre petite fortune avec grand éclat. Nous retournons à présent à Édimbourg pour obtenir une promotion dans notre carrière de comédiens ; et voilà, ma chère cousine, notre histoire. »

Je remerciai l'aimable jeune homme pour son récit divertissant, et après avoir exprimé mes meilleurs vœux de fortune et de bonheur, je les laissai à leur place pour rejoindre mes autres amis qui m'attendaient avec impatience.

Mes aventures approchent de leur fin, ma très chère Marianne ; du moins pour le présent.

À notre arrivée à Édimbourg, Sir Edward me dit qu'en tant que veuve de son fils, il désirait que j'accepte quatre cents livres de rente de sa part. Je promis gracieusement de les recevoir, mais ne pus m'empêcher de remarquer que le baronnet sans cœur me faisait une telle offre plus en raison de mon statut de veuve d'Edward qu'en ma qualité de raffinée et charmante Laura.

Je pris résidence dans un village romantique des Highlands d'Écosse où je demeure depuis, et où je peux, sans être interrompue par des visites inopportunes, me complaire dans la solitude mélancolique de mes incessantes lamentations après la mort de mon père, de ma mère, de mon mari, et de mon amie.

Augusta est depuis plusieurs années unie au seul homme qu'elle méritât, Graham ; elle fit sa connaissance pendant son séjour en Écosse.

Sir Edward, dans l'espoir d'obtenir un héritier à son titre et à sa fortune, épousa dans le même temps Lady Dorothea, dont les souhaits furent ainsi exaucés.

Philander et Gustavus, après s'être bâti une réputation grâce à leurs performances théâtrales à Édimbourg, gagnèrent Covent Garden, où ils sont toujours en représentation sous les noms d'emprunts de Lewis et Quick[1].

Philippa a depuis longtemps payé sa dette à la Nature ; son mari, en revanche, continue de conduire la voiture qui relie Édimbourg à Sterling.

Adieu, ma très chère Marianne,
Laura.

Fin.

---

1. Comédiens londoniens qui ont notamment participé à la première représentation de la comédie de mœurs *The Rivals*, de Richard Brinsley Sheridan, en 1775. (NdT)

Les Trois Sœurs

À Edward Austen Esquire.
Ce roman inachevé lui est respectueusement dédié
par son humble et dévouée servante,

L'Auteur.

Lettre I

Miss Stanhope à Mrs –

Ma chère Fanny,
Il n'est pas de plus heureuse créature au monde que moi, car Mr Watts m'a demandé de l'épouser. Il s'agit de ma première demande en mariage, et je sais à peine comment l'apprécier à sa juste valeur. Quel triomphe sur les Dutton ! Je n'ai nullement l'intention de l'accepter, me semble-t-il, mais puisque je ne suis pas certaine, je lui ai donné une réponse équivoque avant de le quitter. À présent, ma chère Fanny, votre avis m'est indispensable pour savoir quel parti prendre ; afin que vous puissiez juger des mérites de mon prétendant et de la situation, je vais vous en faire la synthèse. C'est un homme d'un âge avancé, environ trente-deux ans, et très laid, tant et si bien que je ne peux souffrir de poser mon regard sur lui. Il est extrêmement désagréable et je le déteste plus que quiconque. Sa fortune

est immense et j'hériterais ainsi d'une rente considérable ; mais il faut savoir qu'il est en excellente santé. En bref, je ne sais que faire. Si je le refuse, il ne m'a pas caché son intention de faire la même demande à Sophia, et si elle refusait à son tour, à Georgiana, et je ne supporterais pas de les voir mariées avant moi. Si je l'accepte, je sais qu'une vie malheureuse m'attend, car il est grincheux et irritable, extrêmement jaloux, et si avare qu'il me sera impossible de vivre en sa compagnie. Il souhaite faire part de l'affaire à Maman, mais j'ai insisté pour qu'il n'en fasse rien, car elle me forcerait à l'épouser quel que soit mon désir ; cependant, c'est probablement déjà chose faite, car il n'accède jamais aux désirs des autres. Je crois que je vais l'accepter. Imaginez mon triomphe si je me mariais avant Sophy, Georgiana, et les Dutton ; d'autre part il promet d'acquérir une nouvelle voiture pour l'occasion, mais sa couleur est un sujet de discorde, car je l'exige bleue à motifs argent, quand lui déclare qu'elle sera chocolat ; et pour me provoquer davantage, il la veut aussi basse que son ancien modèle. Je vous assure que je le refuserai. Il reviendra demain pour ma réponse définitive, alors je crois qu'il me faut l'accepter tant que je le peux. Les Dutton m'envieront et ainsi je pourrai chaperonner Sophy et Georgiana à tous les bals cet hiver. Mais à quoi bon, s'il ne me laisse pas sortir moi-même ? Car je sais qu'il a la danse en horreur, et qu'il ne conçoit pas que d'autres puissent aimer ce qu'il hait ; par ailleurs, il dit sans cesse que la place d'une femme est à la maison, et ce genre de choses. Je crois que je ne puis l'accepter ; je déclinerais immédiatement si j'avais la certitude qu'aucune de mes sœurs ne l'accepte, et que devant leur refus, il ne se tournerait pas vers les Dutton. Je ne puis courir un tel risque, ainsi, s'il promet de commander la voiture que je veux, j'accepterai ; sinon, il pourra bien la conduire seul. J'espère que vous saurez apprécier ma détermination ; je ne puis songer à une meilleure solution.

Pour toujours affectueusement vôtre,
Mary Stanhope

Lettre II

De la même à la même

Chère Fanny,
Je venais de sceller la lettre que je vous adressais quand ma mère entra pour m'annoncer qu'elle devait m'entretenir d'un sujet en particulier.

« Ah ! Je sais de quoi il retourne, dis-je, ce vieux fou de Mr Watts vous a tout rapporté même si je le lui ai interdit. Cependant, vous ne pouvez me forcer à l'accepter.

— Je ne vous forcerai à rien du tout, mon enfant, je souhaite simplement connaître votre résolution et vous rappeler qu'il est impératif de prendre une décision, dans un sens ou dans l'autre, sachant que si vous le refusez, Sophy pourra l'accepter.

— En effet, répondis-je vivement, nul besoin pour Sophy de s'en inquiéter, car je l'épouserai moi-même.

— Si telle est votre décision, dit Mère, pourquoi craindre que je vous l'impose ?

— Mais pardi, parce que je n'ai pas encore choisi de l'accepter ou non.

— Vous êtes l'enfant la plus étrange au monde, Mary. Ce que vous dites un instant, vous le contredisez le suivant. Une bonne fois pour toutes, comptez-vous l'épouser ou non ?

— Enfin ! Maman, comment affirmer ce que je ne sais point ?

— Dans ce cas je vous invite à le savoir, et rapidement, car Mr Watts refuse d'être tenu en haleine.

— Cela ne dépend que de moi.

— Non, certainement pas, car si vous ne lui donnez pas une réponse demain pour le thé, il demandera la main de Sophy.

— Alors je raconterai au monde combien il s'est mal comporté à mon égard.

— Et quel bien cela vous fera-t-il ? Mr Watts a été trop longtemps abusé par le monde pour s'en soucier désormais.

— Si seulement j'avais un père ou un frère qui pouvait le défier !

— Il serait bien mal avisé de le faire, car Mr Watts s'enfuirait sans tarder ; ainsi vous devez décider si oui ou non vous l'acceptez, et ce avant demain soir. Vous n'avez d'autre choix.

— Mais pourquoi, si je ne veux pas de lui, doit-il demander la main de mes sœurs ?

— Pourquoi ! Parce qu'il souhaite s'allier à notre famille et parce qu'elles sont aussi jolies que vous.

— Mais Sophy l'épousera-t-elle, Maman, s'il lui en fait la demande ?

— Certainement. Pourquoi le refuserait-elle ? Mais si elle ne le souhaite pas, Georgiana le devra, car je suis déterminée à ne pas laisser s'échapper une telle opportunité pour mes filles de s'établir si avantageusement. Faites bon usage du temps qu'il vous reste. Je vous laisse régler cette question seule. »

Sur ce, elle me quitta. La seule solution à laquelle je puisse songer, ma chère Fanny, est de demander à Sophy et Georgiana quelle serait leur réponse s'il les demandait en mariage, et si elles me disent qu'elles ne l'épouseraient pas, je suis résolue à le refuser aussi, car je le hais plus que vous ne pouvez l'imaginer. Quant aux Dutton, s'il choisissait d'épouser l'une d'elles, j'aurais la satisfaction de l'avoir refusé la première. Ainsi je vous laisse, ma chère amie.

Éternellement vôtre,

M. S.

Lettre III

Miss Georgiana Stanhope à Miss –

Mercredi

Ma chère Anne,
Sophy et moi nous apprêtons à jouer un tour à notre sœur aînée ; nous n'y sommes pas tout à fait résolues, mais les circonstances sont telles que nous avons des excuses. Notre voisin Mr Watts a demandé la main de Mary – et elle ne sait que répondre, car elle l'abhorre particulièrement (en cela elle n'est pas la seule), et pourtant elle préférerait l'accepter plutôt qu'il n'épouse Sophy ou moi, ce qu'il menace de faire en cas de refus. Vous devez savoir que la pauvre enfant craint par-dessus tout que nous nous mariions avant elle, et pour l'éviter, elle choisirait une misère éternelle en s'unissant à Mr Watts. Il y a de cela une heure, elle est venue nous interroger sur notre sentiment concernant cette affaire, qui allait déterminer le sien. Peu de temps avant, Mère nous en avait fait le récit, déclarant que jamais elle ne le laisserait trouver une épouse en dehors de notre famille. « Ainsi, dit-elle, si Mary ne l'accepte pas, Sophy le fera, et si elle refuse, Georgiana le devra. » Pauvre Georgiana ! Aucune de nous ne tenta d'altérer la résolution de Mère, qui, je regrette de l'admettre, est en général plus inflexible que rationnelle. Dès son départ, cependant,

je rompis le silence pour dire à Sophy que si Mary refusait Mr Watts, je n'attendais pas d'elle qu'elle sacrifie son propre bonheur en devenant son épouse par générosité envers moi – ce que, je le crains, sa bonne nature et son affection fraternelle l'auraient poussée à faire.

« Espérons plutôt, répondit-elle, que Mary ne le refusera point. Pourtant, comment puis-je souhaiter voir ma sœur mariée à un homme qui ne peut la rendre heureuse ?

— Lui ne le peut, c'est vrai, mais sa fortune, son nom, son domaine, sa voiture s'en chargeront, et je suis certaine que Mary l'épousera ; en effet, pourquoi ne le ferait-elle pas ? Il n'a pas plus de trente-deux ans, un âge tout à fait respectable pour le mariage ; il est certes laid, mais qu'est-ce que la beauté chez un homme ? S'il est doté d'une silhouette distinguée et d'un visage sérieux, c'est bien suffisant.

— Tout ceci est fort vrai, Georgiana, mais la silhouette de Mr Watts est malheureusement extrêmement vulgaire, et son expression des plus lourdes.

« Quant à son tempérament, on le dit mauvais, mais le monde ne pourrait-il pas s'être mépris à son sujet ? Il y a une certaine franchise très masculine dans sa disposition. On le dit avare ; appelons cela de la prudence. On le dit soupçonneux. De cela, on peut induire un tempérament fougueux que l'on pardonne toujours chez un jeune homme, et en conclusion, je ne vois pas de raison qui l'empêcherait d'être un bon époux, susceptible de faire le bonheur de Mary. »

Sophy s'esclaffa, et je continuai.

« Cependant, que Mary l'accepte ou non, je suis résolue. Ma décision est prise. Jamais je n'épouserai Mr Watts quand bien même la mendicité serait ma seule alternative. Il laisse tant à désirer, sur bien des aspects ! Si mal fait de sa personne, et sans la moindre qualité pour le racheter. Sa fortune, assurément, est grande. Et pourtant pas si grande en vérité ! Trois mille livres de rente. Que sont trois mille livres de rente ? Ce n'est que six fois le revenu de Mère. Je ne saurais être tentée.

— Pourtant, c'est une noble fortune pour Mary, répondit Sophy en riant encore.

— Pour Mary ! Oui, certainement, cela me procurera un grand plaisir de la voir, elle, si aisée. »

Ainsi poursuivis-je, au plus grand divertissement de ma sœur, jusqu'au moment où Mary entra dans la pièce, en proie à une agitation manifeste. Nous lui fîmes une place auprès du feu. Elle semblait ne pas savoir par où commencer, et finit par dire, de manière quelque peu confuse :

« Dites-moi, Sophy, songez-vous parfois au mariage ?

— Au mariage ! Pas le moins du monde. Mais pourquoi cette question ? Avez-vous connaissance d'un prétendant susceptible de se déclarer ?

— Je... non, comment le saurais-je ? Mais ne puis-je donc pas poser une question ordinaire ?

— Pas si ordinaire, en vérité, Mary.

Elle ne répondit pas, et après quelques instants de silence, reprit :

« Cela vous plairait-il d'épouser Mr Watts, Sophy ? »

Je lançai une œillade à Sophy, et répondis à sa place :

« Qui diable refuserait un mari doté de trois mille livres de rente ?

— En effet, répondit-elle, c'est très juste. Alors, l'accepteriez-vous s'il vous en faisait la demande, Georgiana, et vous-même, Sophy ? »

Sophy n'aimait pas l'idée du mensonge et de la duperie envers sa sœur ; elle s'épargna le premier et sauva à demi sa conscience par une réponse équivoque.

« J'agirais, à n'en pas en douter, de la même façon que Georgiana.

— Dans ce cas, très bien, dit Mary, l'œil brillant d'une lueur de triomphe, sachez que j'ai moi-même reçu une demande en mariage de Mr Watts. »

Notre stupeur fut, bien entendu, des plus grandes.

« Oh ! Ne l'acceptez pas, je vous en conjure, dis-je, ainsi peut-être voudra-t-il de moi. »

En résumé, mon plan fonctionna, et afin de prévenir notre bonheur supposé, Mary est résolue à faire ce qu'elle n'aurait jamais consenti pour notre bonheur réel. Et pourtant mon cœur ne saurait me pardonner, et celui de Sophy est encore plus sévère. Apaisez nos esprits, ma chère Anne, en nous écrivant que vous approuvez notre conduite. Considérez bien l'affaire. Mary prendra un plaisir véritable à accéder au statut de femme mariée, et à nous chaperonner, ce qu'elle s'empressera de faire, et je me crois contrainte de contribuer autant que possible à son bonheur dans l'état que je l'ai poussée à choisir. Ils auront probablement une nouvelle voiture, ce qui la ravira au possible, et si l'on peut obtenir de Mr W. qu'il lui offre également un phaéton, elle sera comblée. Ces choses, en revanche, ne nous seraient à Sophy, ni à moi, d'aucune consolation dans le malheur conjugal. Souvenez-vous-en, et ne nous blâmez pas.

Vendredi

Hier soir, il était convenu que Mr Watts vienne pour le thé. Dès que sa voiture s'arrêta devant la porte, Mary courut à la fenêtre.

« Le croirez-vous, Sophy, s'écria-t-elle, si je vous disais que le vieux fou souhaite faire faire sa nouvelle chaise de la couleur exacte de la précédente, et la fixer tout aussi bas ? C'est impensable, et j'insiste sur ce point. S'il refuse de la bâtir aussi haute que celle des Dutton, et bleue à motifs argent, je le refuserai. Oui, c'est décidé. Le voici qui arrive. Je sais qu'il se montrera grossier ; je sais qu'il fera preuve de mauvaise humeur et ne m'adressera pas le moindre compliment ! Ni ne se comportera le moins du monde comme un amant. »

Elle s'assit et Mr Watts fit son entrée.

« Mesdemoiselles, votre humble serviteur. »

Nous lui offrîmes nos compliments et il s'installa.

« Beau temps, Mesdemoiselles. »

Puis il dit à Mary :

« Bien, Miss Stanhope, j'espère que vous avez enfin réussi à prendre une décision ; et que vous serez assez bonne pour me faire savoir si vous daignez m'épouser ou non.

— Il me semble, monsieur, répondit Mary, que vous auriez pu me le demander d'une façon plus aimable. Je ne sais si un comportement si étrange mérite mon assentiment.

— Mary !

— Eh bien, Maman, s'il se comporte de manière si...

— Chut ! Voyons, Mary, ne manquez pas de respect envers Mr Watts.

— Je vous en prie, madame, ne contraignez pas Miss Stanhope à se montrer courtoise. Si elle ne m'accorde pas sa main, je peux en demander une autre, car je n'ai aucune préférence particulière parmi vos filles : il m'est absolument égal d'épouser l'une des trois. »

Eut-on jamais vu pareil misérable ! Sophy s'empourpra de rage et je sentis monter en moi un mépris immense.

« Très bien, dit Mary d'un ton irrité. J'accepte, puisque vous insistez tant.

— J'aurais cru, Miss Stanhope, qu'aucune violence n'était faite aux sentiments avec des compensations telles que celles que je vous ai offertes. »

Mary marmonna quelques paroles parmi lesquelles je parvins à discerner « à quoi bon être l'héritière d'un mari qui ne se décide pas à mourir ? », puis elle déclara plus distinctement : « Souvenez-vous de mes dépenses ; deux cents à l'année.

— Cent soixante-quinze, madame.

— Deux cents, monsieur, dit Mère.

— Et souvenez-vous, j'aurai une nouvelle voiture aussi haute que celle des Dutton, bleue avec des motifs argent ; et j'attends un nouveau cheval, une parure de dentelle fine, et un nombre infini des plus précieux bijoux. Des diamants exceptionnels, nacres, rubis, émeraudes, et plus de perles qu'on ne peut en compter. Vous devrez vous doter d'un phaéton, que je veux couleur crème et couronné de fleurs en argent ; et quatre des plus beaux chevaux du royaume qui vous serviront à me conduire tous les jours. Ce n'est pas tout. Vous devrez redécorer entièrement votre maison à mon goût, engager deux valets pour me servir, deux bonnes pour m'assister, me laisser agir comme je l'entends, et vous comporter en très bon époux. »

Ici elle s'arrêta, relativement essoufflée, je crois.

« Il est tout à fait raisonnable, Mrs Stanhope, que votre fille soit déçue. »

Il continuait, mais Mary l'interrompit : « Vous devrez me construire une serre élégante, et la remplir de plantes. Me laisser passer chaque hiver à Bath, chaque printemps en ville, chaque été en visite, et chaque automne dans un endroit près de l'eau, et si nous restons à la maison le reste de l'année (Sophy et moi éclatâmes de rire) vous devrez donner bals et mascarades sans cesse. À cette fin vous ferez bâtir une salle et un théâtre où se joueront les pièces. La première que nous donnerons sera *Which is the Man?*, et j'y incarnerai Lady Bell Bloomer.

— Et je vous prie de me dire, Miss Stanhope, dit Mr Watts, ce que je peux attendre de vous en retour de tout ceci ?

— En retour ? Eh bien, en retour, vous pourrez constater mon bon plaisir.

— Le contraire serait bien étrange. Vos attentes, madame, sont bien trop élevées pour moi, et je dois me tourner vers Miss Sophy, qui peut-être n'aura pas tant nourri les siennes.

— Vous vous leurrez, monsieur, en supposant ainsi, dit Sophy, car s'ils ne portent pas tout à fait sur le même objet, mes critères sont absolument aussi exigeants que ceux de ma sœur, puisque j'attends de mon mari qu'il ait le tempérament bon et joyeux ; qu'il prenne mon bonheur en compte à tout moment, et qu'il m'aime avec constance et sincérité. »

Mr Watts la regarda, stupéfait.

« Quelles drôles d'idées, en vérité, jeune fille. Vous feriez mieux de les abandonner avant votre mariage, sans quoi vous serez contrainte de le faire ensuite. »

Mère, entre-temps, avait fait la morale à Mary. Consciente d'être allée trop loin, quand Mr Watts se tourna vers moi dans l'idée, je crois, de me parler, celle-ci s'adressa à lui d'une voix mi-humble, mi-maussade.

« Vous vous êtes mépris, Mr Watts, si vous avez cru à la sincérité de mes requêtes. Mais j'insiste pour avoir une nouvelle voiture.

— Assurément, monsieur, vous conviendrez que Mary est en droit d'en attendre si peu.

— Mrs Stanhope, j'ai l'intention, et je l'ai toujours eue, de faire l'acquisition d'une nouvelle voiture pour mon mariage. Mais elle sera de la couleur de celle que j'ai déjà.

— Je crois, Mr Watts, que vous devez à mon enfant la courtoisie d'entendre son avis sur des questions de cet ordre. »

Mr Watts refusait de céder, et pendant un temps il s'obstina à ne l'envisager que chocolat, tandis que Mary ne démordait pas du bleu à motifs argent. Enfin, Sophy proposa que pour plaire à Mr Watts, on la demande marron foncé, et que pour satisfaire Mary, elle soit haute et décorée d'un liseré argent. L'affaire fut conclue, non sans réticence des deux parties, car chacun entendait arriver à pleine satisfaction. Nous abordâmes ensuite les autres sujets, et il fut décidé qu'ils se marieraient aussi vite que les formalités le permettraient. Mary insistait sur l'obtention d'une licence spéciale signée par l'archevêque de Canterbury en personne, tandis que Mr Watts voulait se contenter de publier les bans. Une licence commune fut enfin négociée. Mary entrera en possession de tous les bijoux de famille (loin d'être considérables, je crois) et Mr Watts promet de lui offrir un cheval ; mais en retour, elle ne doit pas être vue en ville ou dans tout autre lieu public ces trois prochaines années. Elle n'aura ni serre, ni théâtre, ni phaéton, ni valet supplémentaire, et devra se contenter d'une bonne. Ces négociations occupèrent toute la soirée ; Mr Watts resta pour le souper et ne nous quitta pas avant minuit. Sitôt après son départ, Mary s'exclama « Dieu merci ! Il est enfin parti ! Ô combien je le hais ! » C'est en vain que Maman lui expliqua le caractère inapproprié de sa haine envers celui qui allait devenir son mari, car elle persistait à professer son aversion pour lui et à souhaiter ne jamais le revoir. Quelle cérémonie cela augure !

Adieu, ma chère Anne,
Votre fidèle et sincère,

Georgiana Stanhope

Lettre IV

De la même à la même

Samedi

Chère Anne,
Mary, dans sa hâte de partager avec tous la nouvelle de son mariage, et plus particulièrement de son triomphe (comme elle le dit) sur les Dutton, désirait que nous l'accompagnions ce matin à Stoneham. Comme nous n'avions rien d'autre à faire, nous acceptâmes sans tarder et profitâmes d'une promenade aussi plaisante que possible en compagnie de Mary, qui ne fit qu'injurier l'homme qu'elle s'apprêtait à épouser, et se lamenter d'avoir dû renoncer à une voiture bleue à motifs argent. Lorsque nous arrivâmes chez les Dutton, les deux filles se trouvaient dans le vestiaire en compagnie d'un jeune homme, qui nous fut bien entendu présenté. Il était le fils de Sir Henry Brudenell du Leicestershire. Mr Brudenell est le plus bel homme qui m'ait été donné de voir ; il nous enchanta toutes les trois. Mary, qui, depuis notre arrivée dans le vestiaire, s'emplissait de sa propre importance et du désir de la faire connaître, ne put se contraindre au silence trop longtemps après que nous eûmes pris place et s'adressa bientôt à Kitty.

« Ne pensez-vous pas qu'il sera nécessaire d'avoir toutes les parures prêtes ?

— Prêtes pour quoi ?
— Pour quoi ? Mais enfin, pour mon entrée.
— Toutes mes excuses, mais je ne vous comprends pas. De quelles parures est-il question, et à quelle occasion votre entrée sera-t-elle faite ?
— Au prochain bal, bien sûr, après mon mariage. »
Vous imaginerez sans doute leur stupeur. Elles furent tout d'abord incrédules, mais quand nous leur confirmâmes l'histoire, elles admirent sa véracité. « Mais avec qui donc ? » fut évidemment la première question. Mary feignit la timidité, et répondit dans la confusion, le regard baissé, « Mr Watts ». Cette nouvelle requit également une confirmation de notre part, car qu'une jeune fille qui, comme Mary, possédait beauté et fortune (modeste, mais non négligeable) puisse épouser Mr Watts de son plein gré, leur semblait difficile à concevoir. Le sujet ayant été tout à fait introduit, elle se retrouva au centre de toutes les attentions, cessa d'affecter la confusion et quitta sa réserve pour devenir parfaitement expansive.

« Je suis étonnée que vous n'en ayez jamais eu vent, car en général, les choses de cette nature sont très connues du voisinage.

— Je vous assure, dit Jemima, que je n'ai jamais eu de raison de soupçonner une telle affaire. En est-il question depuis longtemps ?

— Oh, oui ! Depuis mercredi. »

Tous sourirent, et particulièrement Mr Brudenell.

« Il vous faut savoir que Mr Watts est très épris de moi, ainsi, c'est un grand mariage d'amour de son côté.

— Pas seulement du sien, je suppose, dit Kitty.

— Oh ! Lorsqu'il y a tant d'amour d'un côté, il n'y en a pas la place de l'autre. Cependant, je ne le hais point trop, même s'il est assurément laid. »

Mr Brudenell demeura ébahi, les Miss Dutton s'esclaffèrent, et Sophy et moi eûmes profondément honte de notre sœur. Elle poursuivit.

« Nous allons avoir une nouvelle chaise de poste, et bientôt très probablement, un phaéton. »

Ce que nous savions être faux, mais la pauvre enfant prenait tant de plaisir à persuader l'assemblée qu'une telle chose allait se produire que je n'osai la priver d'une joie si innocente. Elle continua.

« Mr Watts va m'offrir les bijoux de famille, que j'imagine très considérables. » Je ne pus m'empêcher de murmurer à Sophy « Pas moi ». « Je suppose que ces joyaux doivent être sertis avant d'être portés. Je ne les porterai pas avant le premier bal qui suivra mon mariage. Si Mrs Dutton n'a pas l'intention de s'y rendre, j'espère que vous me laisserez vous y chaperonner ; il ne fait aucun doute que j'y conduirais Sophy et Georgiana.

— Vous êtes trop bonne, dit Kitty, et puisque vous êtes encline à prendre en charge des jeunes filles, je vous conseille de convaincre Mrs Edgecumbe de vous laisser chaperonner ses six filles, qui, ajoutées à vos deux sœurs et à nous-mêmes, rendront votre entrée on ne peut plus respectable. »

Cette réplique nous fit tous sourire sauf Mary, qui, ne comprenant pas le sous-entendu, répondit nonchalamment qu'elle n'apprécierait sûrement pas de chaperonner autant de jeunes filles. Sophy et moi entreprîmes alors de changer de sujet, mais pour quelques minutes seulement, car Mary prit soin d'attirer à nouveau l'attention sur elle et son mariage à venir. Je fus désolée pour ma sœur de constater que Mr Brudenell semblait prendre plaisir à écouter son récit, et même à l'encourager de ses questions et remarques, car il était évident que son unique dessein était d'en rire. J'ai bien peur qu'il ne l'ait trouvée très ridicule. Il sut garder contenance, mais l'on voyait fort bien que c'était au prix de grands efforts. Enfin, il parut las et dégoûté de sa grotesque conversation, car il se tourna plutôt vers nous et lui reparla à peine pendant la demi-heure qui précéda notre départ de Stoneham. Dès que nous quittâmes la maison, nous nous accordâmes à louer la personne et les manières de Mr Brudenell.

Nous trouvâmes Mr Watts chez nous.

« Voyez, Miss Stanhope, dit-il, comme je viens vous faire la cour à la manière d'un véritable amant.

— Vous n'aviez nul besoin de me le dire. J'ai très bien compris la raison de votre venue. »

Sophy et moi quittâmes la pièce, nous imaginant déranger le théâtre d'une cour qui s'apprêtait à débuter. Nous fûmes surprises d'être presque immédiatement rejointes par Mary.

« Avez-vous si vite cessé de vous conter fleurette ? demanda Sophy.

— Que dites-vous ! répondit Mary. Nous nous sommes querellés. Watts n'est qu'un imbécile ! J'espère ne jamais le revoir.

— J'ai bien peur que vous n'y soyez contrainte, dis-je, car il dîne ici aujourd'hui. Mais quel a été le sujet de votre dispute ?

— Eh bien, il a suffi que je lui dise avoir rencontré un homme bien plus beau que lui ce matin pour qu'il s'emporte et me traite de mégère, alors après lui avoir dit qu'il était un bien grossier personnage, je l'ai quitté.

— Simple et concis ; mais dites-moi, Mary, que faire pour réparer cela ?

— Il faudrait qu'il me demande pardon ; mais s'il le faisait, je ne le lui accorderais pas.

« Sa soumission ne serait donc pas d'une grande utilité. »

Une fois apprêtées, nous retournâmes au petit salon où Maman et Mr Watts s'entretenaient. Il semble qu'il s'était plaint du comportement de sa fille, et qu'elle l'avait persuadé d'oublier toute l'affaire. Ainsi, il accueillit Mary avec sa courtoisie coutumière, et à l'exception d'un accroc au sujet du phaéton, et d'un autre sur la serre, l'après-midi se déroula dans la plus grande harmonie. Watts prévoit de se rendre en ville pour hâter les préparatifs du mariage.

Votre amie affectueuse,
G. S.

Jack et Alice

À Francis William Austen Esq., aspirant à bord du navire de Sa Majesté, le Persévérance, *à qui ce roman est dédié par son humble et dévouée servante,*

L'Auteur.

Chapitre I

Un beau jour, Mr Johnson atteignit l'âge de cinquante-trois ans ; dans les douze mois qui suivirent, il en eut cinquante-quatre, ce qui le ravit à tel point qu'il décida de célébrer l'anniversaire suivant en organisant un bal masqué qui rassemblerait ses enfants et ses amis. Ainsi, le jour de ses cinquante-cinq ans, des invitations furent envoyées à tous ses voisins. Notons qu'en ce bas monde, son cercle de relations n'était pas des plus larges, puisqu'il ne comptait que Lady Williams, Mr et Mrs Jones, Charles Adams et les trois Miss Simpson – soit l'ensemble des habitants de Pammydiddle. Tous furent conviés au bal masqué.

Avant que je ne procède au récit de la soirée, il convient de décrire à mon lecteur les personnes et personnages de la société dont il s'apprête à faire la connaissance.

Mr et Mrs Jones apparaissaient tous deux plutôt grands et très versatiles, mais à bien d'autres égards, ils formaient un couple aux manières correctes et au caractère aimable. Charles Adams était un jeune homme plaisant, accompli, et d'une beauté si éblouissante que seul le regard d'un aigle pouvait se poser sur lui sans ciller.

Tout à fait affable dans ses manières et sa disposition, Miss Simpson avait pour seul défaut une ambition infinie. Sa sœur Sukey était envieuse, méprisante et maligne, d'apparence courtaude, grasse et désagréable. La benjamine, Cecilia, se montrait quant à elle parfaitement séduisante, mais trop maniérée pour être charmante.

En Lady Williams, toutes les vertus se concentraient, faisant d'elle une veuve dont la fortune égalait en joliesse les vestiges de ses traits. Généreuse et sincère en dépit de sa bienveillance et de sa franchise ; religieuse et plaisante malgré sa piété et sa bonté ; élégante et aimable, et pourtant raffinée et distrayante.

Au sein de la famille Johnson régnait l'amour, et malgré son goût un peu trop prononcé pour la bouteille et les cartes, on pouvait lui trouver de nombreuses qualités.

Ainsi se composait la société réunie dans l'élégant salon de Johnson Court. Au milieu des loups féminins se distinguaient particulièrement les jolis traits d'une sultane. Parmi la gent masculine, un masque représentant le soleil était, de tous, le plus admiré. Des faisceaux rayonnaient de ses yeux tels ceux du glorieux astre, quoique infiniment supérieurs et si puissants que nul n'osait s'aventurer à moins d'un demi-mile ; lui laissant ainsi l'usage du plus bel espace de la pièce, dont la longueur ne dépassait certainement pas les trois quarts d'un mile, ni la largeur un demi. Le gentleman en question, finissant par trouver la férocité de ses rayons fort peu adaptée au lieu – car ils contraignaient le reste des invités à s'entasser dans le coin opposé de la pièce –, ferma à demi les paupières, permettant ainsi à la compagnie de découvrir Charles Adams, en sobre manteau vert, délivré de tout masque.

Lorsque l'ébahissement général commença à s'estomper, l'attention se porta sur deux dominos[1] d'une humeur exécrable ; chacun était très grand, mais semblait par ailleurs doté de nombreuses qualités.

« Voici Mr et Mrs Jones », conjectura le perspicace Charles.

En effet, il s'agissait bien d'eux.

Personne ne parvenait à deviner l'identité de la sultane ! Cependant, après qu'elle eut déclaré à une splendide Flora étendue en une pose étudiée sur le sofa, un : « Oh, Cecilia, si seulement je pouvais devenir ce que je prétends

---

1. Costume de bal masqué consistant en une robe flottante à capuchon et, par métonymie, personne revêtue d'un domino. (NdT)

être ! », elle fut percée à jour par le génie indéfectible de Charles Adams, qui reconnut en elle l'élégante mais ambitieuse Caroline Simpson, et il supposa – à raison – qu'elle s'était adressée à sa jolie mais maniérée sœur cadette.

On s'avança vers la table de jeux où étaient installées trois personnes vêtues d'une robe de prêtre à capuchon, chacune une bouteille à la main et arborant un air d'intense concentration. Une incarnation de la vertu s'échappa vivement de ce tableau indécent, tandis qu'une petite femme replète, représentant l'envie, s'emparait tour à tour des trois joueurs. Charles Adams, plus brillant que jamais, découvrit bientôt que les trois Johnson occupaient la table, que derrière l'envie se cachait Sukey Simpson, et que la vertu n'était autre que Lady Williams.

On abandonna les loups et les invités se retirèrent dans une autre pièce pour prendre part à une élégante réception joliment orchestrée, après quoi, le vin des Johnson ayant coulé à flots, tous les convives (même la vertu) furent ramenés à bon port, ivres morts.

Chapitre II

Trois mois durant, le bal masqué suffit à alimenter les conversations des habitants de Pammydiddle ; mais aucun personnage ne délia autant les langues que celui de Charles Adams. La singularité de son apparence, les rayons qui avaient jailli de ses yeux, sa vivacité d'esprit et *tutti quanti* avaient tant subjugué le cœur des jeunes filles que parmi les six demoiselles présentes, seules cinq n'étaient pas tombées sous son charme. Alice Johnson était la malheureuse sixième dont le cœur n'avait su résister à ses attraits. Aux lecteurs qu'il surprendra d'apprendre que tant de valeur et d'excellence n'eussent pu conquérir que ce cœur-ci, il leur faut rappeler que ceux des Miss Simpson étaient protégés de tels pouvoirs par l'ambition, l'envie et l'amour de soi.

Aux yeux de Caroline, seuls comptaient les titres de son futur époux ; tandis qu'en Sukey, une telle supériorité n'aurait pu susciter en lieu d'amour que jalousie ; Cecilia entretenait trop d'affection à l'égard de sa propre personne pour se laisser attendrir par une autre. Quant à Lady Williams et Mrs Jones, la première était trop raisonnable pour s'enticher d'un jeune homme de tant d'années son cadet, et la seconde, bien que très grande et irritable, avait trop d'estime pour son mari pour que lui viennent pareils sentiments.

En dépit des efforts de Miss Johnson pour déceler en lui une passion à son égard, le cœur froid et indifférent de Charles Adams conserva, selon toute apparence, sa liberté naturelle ; poli envers tous, n'exprimant de préférence pour aucun, il demeurait le charmant, vivant, mais insensible Charles Adams.

Un soir, Alice se trouvant curieusement troublée par le vin (un état d'une rareté contestable) voulut apaiser son esprit confus et son cœur en mal d'amour en conversant avec l'intelligente Lady Williams.

Sans surprise, elle la trouva chez elle. L'élégante dame n'était pas friande des sorties, et à l'instar du grand Sir Charles Grandison qui ne concevait qu'on puisse refuser les visites, elle méprisait – presque tout autant que la pure bigamie – l'usage en vogue consistant à fermer la porte au nez des visiteurs désagréables.

Hélas, le spiritueux n'avait pas rendu la pauvre Alice spirituelle ; elle ne pouvait penser à rien d'autre qu'à Charles Adams, n'avait que son nom à la bouche, et enfin s'exprima avec tant de franchise que Lady Williams découvrit bientôt l'affection qu'il ne lui rendait pas, ce qui attisa tant sa pitié et sa compassion qu'elle s'adressa à elle en ces termes :

« Je ne perçois que trop clairement, ma chère Miss Johnson, que votre cœur n'a su résister aux attraits de ce jeune homme, et je vous plains sincèrement. S'agit-il de votre premier amour ?

— Oui, madame.

— Je suis d'autant plus peinée de l'apprendre ; étant moi-même un bien triste exemple des malheurs qu'engendre le premier amour, sentiment que j'entends fuir comme la peste à l'avenir. J'espère qu'il n'est pas trop tard pour que vous fassiez de même, auquel cas assurez-vous, ma chère enfant, de vous garder d'un tel danger. Un second attachement implique rarement de sérieuses conséquences. Je ne tenterai donc pas de vous en protéger. Méfiez-vous du premier amour, et vous n'aurez nul besoin d'en craindre un second.

— Vous dites, madame, avoir été vous-même victime du malheur que vous êtes assez bonne pour me souhaiter de ne jamais rencontrer. Me ferez-vous l'honneur du récit de votre vie et de vos aventures ?

— Bien volontiers, ma chère. »

Chapitre III

« Mon père était un gentleman à la tête d'une fortune considérable dans le Berkshire, avec pour seuls héritiers ses enfants. J'eus le malheur de perdre ma mère dès mes six ans ; eu égard à mon âge jeune et tendre, mon père, au lieu de m'envoyer en pension, trouva une gouvernante à même de superviser mon éducation à la maison. Mes frères furent placés dans des écoles appropriées et mes sœurs, toutes plus jeunes que moi, demeurèrent sous la garde de leur nourrice.

« Miss Dickins était une excellente gouvernante. Elle m'enseigna les chemins de la vertu ; sous son instruction, chaque jour je devins plus aimable, et peut-être aurais-je frôlé la perfection, si ma fidèle préceptrice ne m'avait pas été arrachée le jour où j'atteignis ma dix-septième année. Jamais je n'oublierai ses derniers mots : "Ma chère Kitty, bonne nuit." Jamais plus je ne la revis, continua Lady Williams en épongeant ses larmes. Elle nous quitta avec le valet ce même soir.

« L'année qui suivit, une cousine distante de mon père m'invita à passer l'hiver avec elle en ville. Mrs Watkins était une dame de rang, de richesse, et de renom. On la disait jolie, mais personnellement, je n'ai jamais trouvé sa beauté remarquable. Son front était trop haut, ses yeux trop petits, et elle avait trop de couleur.

— Comment cela est-il possible ? l'interrompit Miss Johnson, s'empourprant de colère. Pensez-vous que l'on puisse avoir trop de couleur ?

— En effet, je le crois, et je vais vous dire pourquoi, ma chère Alice. Lorsqu'une personne est dotée d'un excès de rouge dans son teint, cela lui confère, à mon humble opinion, une allure trop rouge.

— Mais un visage peut-il, madame, avoir une allure trop rouge ?

— Assurément, ma chère Miss Johnson, et en voici la raison : quand un visage a une allure trop rouge, il n'est pas autant à son avantage que s'il avait été plus pâle.

— Je vous en prie, madame, poursuivez votre histoire.

— Eh bien, comme je vous le disais plus tôt, cette dame m'invita à lui rendre visite pour quelques semaines. Nombre de messieurs la trouvaient belle, mais à mon avis, son front était bien trop haut, ses yeux trop petits, et elle avait trop de couleur.

— En cela, je demeure d'avis que madame a dû se méprendre. Il est impossible que Mrs Watkins ait été trop colorée, puisqu'une telle chose n'existe point.

— Pardonnez-moi, ma chère, si je ne vous rejoins pas sur ce point. Permettez-moi de m'expliquer clairement. Voici mon idée : lorsqu'une femme possède une trop grande proportion de rouge sur les joues, c'est qu'elle est trop colorée.

— Mais, madame, je refuse de croire qu'il est possible pour quiconque d'avoir sur les joues une trop grande proportion de rouge.

— Comment, ma chère ! Même en étant trop colorée ? »

Miss Johnson commençait d'autant plus à perdre patience que Lady Williams demeurait si froidement inflexible. Il convient de garder en mémoire, cependant, que l'élégante lady avait sur ce point un avantage indéniable – contrairement à Alice, elle n'était pas ivre. Eût-elle senti les effets du vin et de la passion qu'elle n'aurait pu garder son calme.

La dispute finit par tant s'enflammer du côté d'Alice que des mots, elle manquait d'en venir aux mains quand, par chance, M. Johnson entra, et non sans quelques difficultés l'entraîna loin de Lady Williams et des joues rouges de Mrs Watkins.

Chapitre IV

Mes lecteurs imagineront peut-être qu'après un tel fracas, aucune amitié ne pouvait persister entre les Johnson et Lady Williams, mais en cela ils se trompent ; car l'élégante lady était trop raisonnable pour garder rancune d'une conduite qu'elle ne pouvait qu'attribuer aux conséquences naturelles de l'ébriété, et Alice éprouvait un respect trop sincère à l'égard de Lady Williams – et un amour trop grand pour son bordeaux – pour ne pas faire toutes les concessions qui s'imposaient.

Quelques jours après leur réconciliation, Lady Williams rendit visite à Miss Johnson et lui proposa une promenade dans le verger de citronniers qui séparait la porcherie de madame des écuries de Charles Adams. Alice, reconnaissante de cette généreuse proposition, et comblée par la perspective d'apercevoir une écurie appartenant à Charles, accepta avec un plaisir évident. Peu de temps après le début de leur promenade, Lady Williams l'arracha à la contemplation de ce bonheur futur, en lui tenant ce discours :

« Ma chère Alice, si je me suis retenue jusqu'alors de poursuivre le récit de ma vie, c'est pour vous épargner le souvenir d'une scène qui – puisqu'elle vous discrédite plus qu'elle vous honore – ferait mieux d'être oubliée que remémorée. »

Alice, déjà empourprée, s'apprêta à parler, mais percevant sa contrariété, Lady Williams poursuivit sans lui en laisser le temps :

« J'ai peur, ma chère enfant, de vous avoir offensée à l'instant ; je vous assure que mon dessein n'est point de vous froisser en ravivant ce qu'il est trop tard pour corriger. Toutes choses bien considérées, je ne vous blâme pas autant que d'autres le pourraient ; car lorsqu'une personne se trouve sous l'emprise de la liqueur, nul ne peut alors répondre de son comportement.

— Madame, ceci m'est insupportable, j'insiste pour...

— Ma chère enfant, ne vous offusquez point. Je vous assure avoir entièrement oublié le moindre détail de cette affaire ; d'ailleurs, loin d'être irritée ce soir-là, j'avais immédiatement compris que vous étiez presque ivre morte. Je savais que vous ne pouviez vous empêcher de professer des inanités. Mais je perçois votre trouble, je changerai donc de sujet en souhaitant qu'il ne soit jamais plus mentionné. Souvenez-vous que tout est oublié. Je vais maintenant reprendre mon histoire ; mais il me faut insister : je ne vous donnerai point de description de Mrs Watkins. Cela ne ferait que raviver de vieilles histoires, et puisque vous ne l'avez jamais vue, vous ne pouvez vous rendre compte à quel point son front était trop haut, ses yeux trop petits, et son teint – et j'insiste, car il l'était – trop coloré.

— Encore ! Lady Williams, c'en est trop ! »

Cette querelle ainsi ravivée provoqua tant la pauvre Alice que je ne sais ce qu'il serait advenu si elles ne s'étaient pas trouvées distraites par un événement qui attira leur attention. Une jolie jeune femme, visiblement en proie à la douleur et étendue au pied d'un citronnier, représentait une attraction bien trop curieuse pour ne pas capter leur regard. Oubliant leur dispute, animées par la même tendresse compatissante, elles s'avancèrent vers l'inconnue et l'abordèrent ainsi :

« Vous semblez, belle nymphe, souffrir d'un malheur dont nous serions ravies de vous soulager, si vous nous en faisiez part. Vous ferez-nous l'honneur de nous conter les aventures de votre vie ?

— Volontiers, mesdames, si vous acceptez de prendre place à mes côtés. »

Elles s'assirent et écoutèrent son histoire.

Chapitre V

« Je suis née au nord du pays de Galles, dont mon père est l'un des tailleurs des plus réputés. À la tête d'une famille nombreuse, il se laissa aisément persuader par une sœur de ma mère, veuve et heureuse propriétaire d'une taverne dans le village voisin, de la laisser m'élever à ses propres frais. Ainsi vécus-je huit années de ma vie, pendant lesquelles elle me procura les meilleurs maîtres, qui m'enseignèrent tous les accomplissements requis pour une personne de mon sexe et de mon rang. Sous leur tutelle, j'appris la danse, la musique, le dessin, et plusieurs langues étrangères, devenant ainsi la plus accomplie des filles de tailleur de tout le pays de Galles. Jamais on ne vit plus heureuse créature que moi, jusqu'à il y a quelques mois – mais j'aurais dû préciser que le principal domaine de notre voisinage appartient à Charles Adams, le propriétaire de la demeure de briques que vous voyez là-bas.

— Charles Adams ! s'exclama Alice, stupéfaite. Vous connaissez Charles Adams ?

— À mon grand regret, madame, je le confesse. Il y a peut-être six mois, il vint collecter la rente de ladite propriété. C'est à cette occasion que je le vis pour la première fois. Vous semblez, madame, avoir déjà fait sa connaissance, je n'ai donc nul besoin de vous décrire ses charmes. Il me fut impossible de leur résister…

— Ah ! Qui le pourrait ? dit Alice avec un profond soupir.

— Ma tante, ayant lié la plus grande intimité avec sa cuisinière, entreprit à ma demande de découvrir, par le biais de son amie, s'il existait la moindre chance que mon affection soit partagée. C'est dans ce dessein qu'elle alla un soir prendre le thé avec Mrs Susan, qui, au cours de la conversation, mentionna le plaisir que lui procuraient une si bonne place et un si bon maître. Ma tante la pressa avec tant d'habileté que Susan lui confia bientôt qu'à son avis, son maître ne se marierait jamais "car, dit-elle, il déclare encore et encore que sa future épouse devrait impérativement posséder jeunesse, beauté, naissance, esprit, mérite, et fortune. J'ai plus d'une fois, continua-t-elle, entrepris de le raisonner et de le convaincre de l'improbabilité de l'existence d'une telle femme, mais mes arguments n'eurent aucun effet, et il demeure déterminé". Vous imaginerez, mesdames, le désarroi qui m'accabla à ces mots, car je craignais que malgré ma jeunesse, ma beauté, mon esprit, mon mérite et mon statut d'héritière probable de la demeure et de l'affaire de ma tante, il me trouvât déficiente en rang, et estime que par conséquent, je ne mérite pas sa main.

« Cependant, j'étais déterminée à me montrer audacieuse, et ainsi je lui écrivis une très belle lettre, lui offrant avec une grande tendresse mon cœur, et ma main. Sur quoi je reçus un refus fâché et péremptoire. Soupçonnant qu'il s'agissait simplement de l'effet de sa pudeur, je le pressai à nouveau sur le sujet. Mais il ne répondit plus à aucune de mes missives, et très vite, quitta le pays. Dès que j'appris la nouvelle de son départ, je lui écrivis ici, l'informant que je me ferais bientôt l'honneur de lui rendre visite à Pammydiddle, à quoi je ne reçus aucune réponse. Qui ne dit mot consent, j'en suis convaincue, aussi je quittai le pays de Galles à l'insu de ma tante, et arrivai ici ce matin après un périple éprouvant. Quand je demandai après sa demeure, on me recommanda de couper par ces bois jusqu'à celle que vous avez sous les yeux. Le cœur allégé par l'heureuse perspective de le contempler à nouveau, je m'y aventurai, et j'arrivais ici dans mon chemin lorsque je me trouvai soudain attrapée par la jambe. En examinant la cause, je découvris un de ces pièges de fer qui parsèment si souvent les terres des messieurs.

— Ah ! s'écria Lady Williams. Comme il est heureux que nous vous ayons trouvée, sans quoi nous aurions risqué de connaître la même mésaventure !

— C'est, en effet, fort heureux pour vous, mesdames, que je vous aie précédées de peu. Comme vous pouvez l'imaginer, je m'époumonai jusqu'à ce qu'une des servantes de ce misérable sans cœur vienne à mon secours et me délivre de cette affreuse prison, mais pas avant que ma jambe ne soit complètement brisée. »

Chapitre VI

Après un récit si tragique, les beaux yeux de Lady Williams s'étaient emplis de larmes, et Alice ne put contenir une exclamation.

« Oh ! Comme Charles est cruel, de blesser ainsi les cœurs et les jambes innocents ! »

Lady Williams fit remarquer qu'il fallait apporter à la jambe de la jeune demoiselle des soins sans plus tarder. Après un examen de la fracture, elle se lança donc avec compétence dans une opération, ce qui était d'autant plus merveilleux qu'il s'agissait de sa première. Lucy se leva alors d'un bond, et se découvrant à nouveau capable de marcher avec aisance, les accompagna à la demeure de Lady Williams, sur son invitation expresse.

La silhouette parfaite, le beau visage et les élégantes manières de Lucy gagnèrent tant l'affection d'Alice que lorsqu'elles se quittèrent, ce qui n'arriva pas avant la fin du souper, cette dernière lui assura qu'à l'exception de son père, de ses frères, de ses oncles, tantes, cousins, et autres parents, de Lady Williams, Charles Adams, et de quelques dizaines d'amis proches, elle n'aimait personne dans le monde entier autant qu'elle.

Une déclaration si flatteuse aurait procuré un très grand plaisir à son objet, si elle-même n'avait pas lucidement remarqué que la très affectueuse Alice avait profité un peu trop généreusement du bordeaux de Lady Williams.

Cette dernière – grâce à ses grandes qualités de discernement – lut dans la contenance intelligente de Lucy ses pensées sur la question, et dès que Miss Johnson les eut quittées, elle lui dit :

« Quand vous aurez mieux fait connaissance avec mon Alice, ne soyez pas surprise, Lucy, de constater que cette chère créature boit un peu trop ; ce sont des incidents quotidiens. Elle est dotée de nombreuses qualités rares et charmantes, mais la sobriété n'en fait pas partie. Sa famille au complet compose d'ailleurs un bien triste lot d'ivrognes. Je suis tout aussi navrée de vous confier n'avoir jamais vu plus grands amateurs de jeu qu'eux, et Alice en particulier. Mais c'est une jeune fille délicieuse. Non qu'elle ait bon caractère – je l'ai vue en proie à des passions si violentes ! Cependant, c'est une agréable jeune femme. Je suis sûre que vous l'aimerez beaucoup. Je connais très peu de personnes aussi aimables. Oh, mais vous l'auriez vue ce soir-là ! Comme elle s'est emportée ! À propos d'une bagatelle, qui plus est ! Véritablement une jeune fille des plus agréables ! Je lui vouerai toujours une sincère tendresse.

— À en croire le récit de Madame, elle semble pourvue de nombreuses qualités, répondit Lucy.

— Oh ! Quantité, répondit Lady Williams, j'ai énormément d'affection pour elle, bien qu'il ne soit pas impossible que mes sentiments m'aient rendue aveugle à ses véritables défauts. »

Chapitre VII

Le lendemain matin, Lady Williams reçut avec la plus grande courtoisie la visite des trois Miss Simpson et leur présenta Lucy. L'aînée s'en trouva enchantée au point de déclarer que son unique ambition serait de la persuader de les accompagner le matin suivant à Bath, où elles comptaient séjourner plusieurs semaines.

« Lucy, répondit Lady Williams, est tout à fait libre de ses déplacements, et si elle choisissait d'accepter une invitation si aimable, j'espère qu'elle n'hésiterait pas par délicatesse à mon égard. Elle n'est jamais allée à Bath et ce serait sans doute une sortie très agréable pour elle. Parlez, mon enfant, continua-t-elle en se tournant vers Lucy. Que dites-vous d'accompagner ces demoiselles ? Je serai inconsolable en votre absence – ce sera une visite charmante pour vous – j'espère que vous accepterez ; si vous le faites soyez assurée que j'en serai anéantie – je vous en prie, laissez-vous persuader. »

Lucy déclina l'honneur de les accompagner, en se répandant en excuses et en remerciements. Miss Simpson ne cacha point sa déception. Lady Williams insista pour qu'elle accepte, déclarant que sans quoi, elle ne le lui pardonnerait jamais, mais auquel cas, elle-même n'y survivrait pas ; en bref, elle eut recours à des arguments si convaincants qu'il fut enfin décidé qu'elle irait. Les sœurs Simpson vinrent la chercher à dix heures le lendemain et Lady Williams eut bientôt la satisfaction d'apprendre que sa jeune amie était bien arrivée à Bath.

Revenons-en à présent au héros de ce roman, le frère d'Alice, dont je crois avoir à peine eu l'occasion de parler – sans doute en raison de sa fâcheuse propension à la liqueur, qui le priva complètement de toutes les facultés dont la nature l'avait doté, si bien qu'il n'accomplit jamais rien qui valût la peine d'être mentionné. Répercussion naturelle de sa pernicieuse habitude, il mourut peu après le départ de Lucy. Son décès fit de sa sœur l'unique héritière d'une très grosse fortune, ce qui, en lui fournissant un nouvel espoir de satisfaire les critères de Charles Adams, ne put être que source de joie – et puisque la conséquence était heureuse, on ne pouvait en pleurer la cause.

Constatant que la violence de ses sentiments ne cessait de croître, Alice en fit part à son père et lui demanda de proposer une union à Charles. Son père consentit et se décida un matin à toucher un mot de l'affaire au jeune homme. Mr Johnson étant un homme peu loquace, sa tâche fut vite accomplie et il reçut la réponse qui suit.

« Monsieur, on attendrait certainement de moi que j'exprime bonheur et gratitude devant cette proposition, mais permettez-moi de vous dire qu'elle est à mes yeux un affront. Je pense être, monsieur, d'une beauté parfaite – où trouver silhouette plus fine ou visage plus charmant ? Par ailleurs, monsieur, je conçois mes manières et ma prestance comme étant des plus raffinées ; elles possèdent une certaine élégance et une douceur toute particulière que je n'ai jamais vues égalées et que je ne saurais décrire. Sans vouloir être partial, je suis assurément plus accompli dans chaque langue, chaque science, chaque art, et en toute chose, que n'importe qui en Europe. Mon caractère est égal, mes vertus indénombrables, et ma personne exceptionnelle. Puisqu'il en va ainsi, monsieur, de moi, qu'entendez-vous accomplir en souhaitant me voir épouser votre fille ? Laissez-moi vous dresser un rapide portrait de vous et d'elle. Je vous vois, monsieur, comme appartenant à une honnête catégorie d'homme, de manière générale ; vous êtes un vieil ivrogne, c'est certain, mais cela m'importe peu. Votre fille, monsieur, n'est ni assez belle, ni assez plaisante, ni assez spirituelle, ni assez riche pour moi. Je n'attends rien de plus de mon épouse que ce qu'elle trouvera en moi – la perfection. Voici donc, monsieur, mon sentiment, et il est tout à mon honneur. J'ai une amie, et je me félicite de n'en avoir qu'une. Elle est en ce moment occupée à préparer mon dîner, mais si vous le souhaitez, elle viendra vous assurer qu'il s'agit bien là du fond de ma pensée. »

Mr Johnson, satisfait, se déclara bien gré à Mr Adams pour le portrait qu'il avait dressé de sa fille et de lui-même, puis prit congé.

La malheureuse Alice, en entendant le triste récit que lui fit son père de sa visite infructueuse, put à peine supporter une telle déception. Elle se rua sur sa bouteille, et tout fut bientôt oublié.

Chapitre VIII

Tandis qu'à Pammydiddle on réglait ces affaires, à Bath, Lucy rencontrait un franc succès. Quinze jours de villégiature avaient presque effacé de sa mémoire l'image captivante de Charles. Le souvenir des souffrances infligées à son cœur par ses charmes et à sa jambe par son piège lui permit de l'oublier sans trop de peine, ce qu'elle était bien décidée à faire ; et dans ce but, elle employait cinq minutes de chaque jour à l'effacer de sa mémoire.

Sa deuxième lettre à Lady Williams lui annonçait qu'elle avait accompli cette tâche à la perfection ; elle mentionnait également une demande en mariage reçue du duc de —, un homme âgé à la noble fortune et dont la mauvaise santé était la principale raison de son séjour à Bath.

« Je suis tourmentée, poursuivit-elle, de ne pas savoir si je souhaite l'accepter ou non. Il y a des milliers d'avantages à une union avec le duc, car en sus des bagatelles comme le rang et la fortune, il me procurerait un toit, ce qui, de tout, est ce que je désire avec le plus de ferveur. L'aimable souhait de Madame de me voir toujours à vos côtés est noble et généreux, mais il m'est impensable de devenir un si lourd fardeau pour un être que j'apprécie et que j'estime tant. L'idée que ne nous sont obligés que ceux que l'on méprise est un sentiment répandu dans mon esprit par ma tante dès le plus jeune âge, et ne peut, à mon avis, être trop prise au sérieux. L'excellente femme dont je parle est, me dit-on, trop furieuse depuis mon imprudent départ du pays de Galles pour accepter de me revoir un jour. Je souhaite sincèrement quitter les demoiselles avec qui je séjourne à présent. Si Miss Simpson est en effet (ambition mise à part) très aimable, sa sœur, l'envieuse et méchante Sukey, est trop détestable. J'ai des raisons de penser que l'admiration dont j'ai fait l'objet dans les cercles des grands de cet endroit a suscité sa haine et sa jalousie ; car elle m'a souvent menacée, et a parfois tenté de me trancher la gorge. Madame comprendra donc mon désir de quitter Bath, et de trouver un foyer pour m'accueillir. J'attends avec impatience vos conseils concernant le duc et vous suis obligée, etc.

Lucy. »

Lady Williams lui fit part son opinion de la manière qui suit.

« Au sujet du duc, pourquoi, ma très chère Lucy, hésitez-vous ? Je me suis enquise de sa personne, et j'en ai conclu qu'il était un individu sans principes et illettré. Jamais je ne tolérerai que ma Lucy s'unisse à un tel homme ! Il dispose d'une fortune princière, qui chaque jour s'accroît. Comme vous la dépenseriez majestueusement ! Quelle valeur lui donneriez-vous ainsi aux yeux de tous ! Comme il serait respecté grâce à son épouse ! Mais pourquoi, ma très chère Lucy, pourquoi ne consentez-vous pas immédiatement à me revenir pour ne jamais plus me quitter ? Bien que j'admire votre noble sentiment vis-à-vis du respect des obligations, permettez-moi de vous supplier de ne pas le laisser interférer avec mon bonheur. Vous avoir à mes côtés engendrera très certainement de grands frais pour moi – auxquels je ne saurais faire face – mais qu'est-ce en comparaison de la félicité dont je jouirai en votre compagnie ? Cela me ruinera, je le sais – ainsi, assurément, vous ne résisterez pas à mes arguments, ni ne refuserez de revenir à votre affectueusement, etc., etc.

C. Williams. »

Chapitre IX

Nul ne saura jamais l'effet des conseils de Lady Williams, s'ils avaient été reçus par Lucy, car ils parvinrent à Bath quelques heures après qu'elle eut poussé son dernier soupir. Elle avait succombé en martyre à la jalousie et à la malveillance de Sukey, qui, envieuse de ses charmes supérieurs, l'avait arrachée par le poison, à l'âge de dix-sept ans, au monde qui l'admirait.

Ainsi s'éteignit l'aimable et charmante Lucy, dont la vie n'avait été noircie par aucun crime, dont la seule faute avait été son départ imprudent de chez sa tante, et qui fut sincèrement pleurée par toutes ses connaissances. Parmi ses amis les plus affligés, on comptait Lady Williams, Miss Johnson et le duc ; les deux premières avaient eu la plus grande estime pour elle, en particulier Alice, qui avait passé une soirée entière en sa compagnie et n'avait plus songé à elle depuis. On put témoigner tout aussi facilement du chagrin de sa Grâce, puisqu'il perdit une jeune femme pour laquelle il avait éprouvé, depuis dix jours, une tendre affection et une sincère estime. Il pleura sa perte avec une constance inébranlable pendant la quinzaine qui suivit, après quoi il combla l'ambition de Caroline Simpson en l'élevant au rang de duchesse. Ainsi connut-elle un bonheur parfait en assouvissant sa plus grande passion. Sa sœur, la perfide Sukey, fut bien vite récompensée comme de juste par un destin que toutes ses actions trahissaient comme un désir profond. Son crime barbare fut découvert, et malgré toutes les interventions de ses amis, elle fut sans tarder envoyée à la potence. La belle mais maniérée Cecilia était trop sensible à ses propres charmes pour ne pas concevoir que, si Caroline pouvait épouser un duc, elle-même pouvait aspirer sans censure à l'affection d'un prince – et sachant que tous ceux de son pays de naissance étaient déjà fiancés, elle quitta l'Angleterre ; on m'apprit depuis qu'elle était devenue la sultane favorite d'un grand Moghol.

De leur côté, les habitants de Pammydiddle furent plongés dans un grand état de stupéfaction et d'émerveillement, car la nouvelle courut des noces prochaines de Charles Adams. Le nom de l'élue était gardé secret. Mr et Mrs Jones crurent qu'il s'agissait de Miss Johnson ; mais cette dernière, mieux informée, concentrait toutes ses craintes sur la cuisinière quand, à la surprise générale et à la vue de tous, il épousa Lady Williams.

Fin

Achevé d'imprimer en Espagne
par BlackPrint CPI Ibérica S.L.
Sant Andreu de la Barca (08740)
Dépôt légal : mai 2017